"Dr. Komrad's book is an important, much-needed reference that offers the necessary toolbox to ensure the proper treatment and diagnosis of a loved one."

— Patrick J. Kennedy, former member of Congress,
author of the Mental Health Parity and Addiction Equity Act,
and cofounder of One Mind for Research

"My family did a fantastic job with handling the challenge of being related to me, but I think it would have made their burden much lighter if they'd had a book like this."

— Carrie Fisher, author and actress

"This is an authoritative and smart guide for the perplexed in need of care, written by an experienced clinician and teacher."

— Steven S. Sharfstein, M.D.,
clinical professor of psychiatry, University of Maryland

"How do I get my child/spouse/friend to see someone? *This is the most common question psychiatrists hear from families. I recommend this book to all of you in this predicament."*

— J. Raymond DePaulo, Jr., M.D.,
Henry Phipps professor and director, Department of Psychiatry
and Behavioral Sciences, Johns Hopkins Hospital

EUR

A Step-by-Step Plan to
Convince a Loved One to Get Counseling

MARK S. KOMRAD, M.D.

HAZELDEN®

Hazelden
Center City, Minnesota 55012
hazelden.org

Library of Congress Cataloging-in-Publication Data

Komrad, Mark S., 1957-
  You need help! : a step-by-step plan to convince a loved one to get counseling / Mark S. Komrad.
      p. cm.
  Includes bibliographical references.
  ISBN 978-1-61649-148-2 (softcover) — ISBN 978-1-61649-455-1 (ebook)
  1. Mental health counseling. 2. Persuasion (Psychology) 3. Mental illness —Diagnosis. I. Title.
  RC466.K66 2012
  616.89—dc23

                                                                2012012917

Editor's note

The names, details, and circumstances may have been changed to protect the privacy of those mentioned in this publication.

This publication is not intended as a substitute for the advice of health care professionals.

16 15 14 13 12   1 2 3 4 5 6

Cover design by Theresa Jaeger Gedig

Interior design and typesetting by Kinne Design

For my patients, who taught me everything in this book,
and my family—the "psychiatrist's psychiatrist"

"I found [mental health treatment] to be one of the healthiest experiences of my life. I grew up in a working-class family where that was very frowned upon. So it was very, very difficult for me to ever get to a place where I said I needed some help. You know, I stumbled into some different, very dark times where I simply had no other idea of what to do. It's not necessarily for everybody maybe, but all I can say is, I've lived a much fuller life. I've accomplished things personally that felt simply impossible previously. It's a sign of strength, you know, to put your hand out and ask for help, whether it's a friend or a professional or whatever."

— Bruce Springsteen

"Not everything that is faced can be changed, but nothing can be changed until it is faced."

— James Baldwin

Contents

Foreword

Since I first began campaigning for my husband for political office, I have been interested and involved with people who have suffered from mental health problems as well as their families and the communities in which they live. I've written books about how effective the treatment for these problems has become but how difficult access to that treatment can be. As the President's Commission on Mental Health informed my husband back in 1979, so many people who would benefit from it are not getting mental health care. For some, this is because of where they live; for others, it's because of who they are. Reaching out for help, however, is sometimes the most difficult step. Often, people don't know how or when or even whether to seek help. It may be that others—family, friends, coworkers—are the first to see that someone is troubled and could benefit from seeing a trained professional in order to understand the nature of the problem and how it can be addressed. Our children, the elderly, our incredibly stressed veterans, those whose lives have been crushed by economic setbacks or disaster, those raised in hardship, or those who have inherited mental illness—all need to have some way to get started, some assistance to reach out for help and begin their process of recovery.

If you are that family member or friend who first really grasps that someone may be in emotional trouble, this book can give you sound guidance about how to approach the individual. There are so many reasons why he or she may not believe or be aware that there is a problem, or perhaps doesn't want any kind of professional help, or simply may not know how or where to start.

The father of medicine, Hippocrates, wrote over 2,400 years ago: "diagnosis is half the cure." Comprehending the problem is the first step in the journey to recovery. Modern psychiatric treatment starts with trying to determine that knowledge. Since I first got involved in mental health advocacy, much more has been learned about the brain and mind to further our understanding of how someone's mental life becomes troubled and what to do about it. So, that first step—getting to a professional who can begin to sort things out, do an evaluation, make a proper diagnosis, and get treatment started in the right direction—is crucial.

Much can stand in the way of getting professional mental health treatment. I've been working for years trying to improve access for people to get the help they need. At the most basic level, though, it starts with the troubled person in your life: the reason you have picked up this book. This person may be more or less agreeable to getting help, more or less aware that there is a problem. Sometimes all it takes is kind, supportive guidance. Sometimes it may take greater efforts at persuasion or mobilizing outside assistance.

Dr. Komrad has guided thousands of people (and those who care about them) in the process of taking the first step to getting a mental health evaluation and has spoken about it often on his radio show. His book will start you off with the simplest and more supportive approaches. If these don't work, he guides you toward stronger measures, as appropriate. Dr. Komrad points out the resources that are available within families, communities, and even in the courts.

We have come a long way in the understanding and treatment of mental disorders since I chaired the President's Commission on Mental Health in 1979. But we still have a way to go, and every effort is important. After all the policy discussions, legislation, and advocacy, it comes down to one person at a time starting down the path of evaluation, treatment, and recovery. Helping someone to get a proper assessment by meeting with a mental health professional is vital, even blessed work. I believe this book can help you do that work.

— Rosalynn Carter,
  former First Lady of the United States

Acknowledgments

I would like to acknowledge the invaluable assistance of my "book doctor," Martha Murphy. I am a professional psychiatrist, but not a trained writer. Martha has schooled me in the craft of book writing, helped me navigate the strange world of publishing, and provided the kind of developmental editing that helped make this, my first book, more accessible to readers. My agent, Linda Konner, helped me make the invaluable connection with Hazelden Publishing. My wife, Kim, herself an experienced editor, gave the same glow to this manuscript that she brings to my life in general. I am grateful to Steve Sharfstein, M.D., for his mentorship, for his belief in this project, and for introducing me to Rosalynn Carter, who graciously wrote the foreword to this book. Her life's work, advocating for people who need psychiatric treatment, inspires me. Finally, I appreciate my editor, Sid Farrar, at Hazelden, who helped to transform a manuscript that should be read into a book that is worth reading.

Introduction

"The only end of writing is to enable the readers
to enjoy a better life, or better to endure it."
— SAMUEL JOHNSON

In the 1990s, I had a radio show on the American Radio Network called *Komrad on Call*, which was syndicated nationally. It was a call-in show, and my conversations with on-air guests and callers covered the spectrum of psychological concerns. Over the course of the show's four-year run, the single-most-common call-in question went something like this: *My sister* [brother/husband/wife/child/ colleague at work] *is clearly experiencing some real emotional problems. I think she needs psychiatric help. How do I broach the subject?*

In my private practice, too, this has been a frequent query. And in social settings, I am often approached by someone who, in a low tone, poses the same question. I came to see that a need existed, and the seeds for this book were planted.

When you are worried about someone in your life, someone whose life is in a downward spiral, you may be struggling with this same quandary. You may have tried to help and been rebuffed; or you've helped and things *did* get better for a while, but now you see the old patterns reemerging. Maybe you haven't said anything because you

1

don't know what to say or fear a negative response ("Are you telling me I'm crazy?") if you suggest a mental health professional might be helpful. Are these problems beyond your capacities as a friend, spouse, colleague, or relative? What *can* you do?

If you have reached this point with a loved one, a roommate, a friend—the point where you know he or she has problems beyond your ability to remedy and it's time for professional help—I'm glad you're here. This book will give you the understanding and tools to help your friend get what is so obviously needed—a consultation with a mental health professional.

As a psychiatrist in practice for twenty-five years, I meet with people who have concerns just like yours. They want to help someone, but they aren't sure whether to get involved, how to get involved, or how to help. During my years in practice, I have not only helped people with their own mental health problems but also coached caring people who want to know how to help a troubled friend or relative.

When I recall dramatic mental illness stories in the media, I am repeatedly struck by how often friends and family had observed the person become increasingly troubled, knew that this was abnormal, figured *something* was wrong in that person's mental life, but didn't say anything, do anything, or consult with anybody else about what they were seeing. The silence in these onlookers has always struck me as deafening. A caller to one radio show after the Tucson massacre where Congresswoman Gabrielle Giffords was shot described how her own son had a psychotic break at age eighteen. Later, when she spoke to his friends, they confessed they had seen the emergence of hallucinations and delusions in her son for a couple of months, but never told his parents, or anyone else. He was showing things to his friends that he was able to hide from his family, but those friends said nothing. I had to write this book because I came to understand that one of the major missing pieces in approaching people with psychiatric problems is the efforts of friends and loved ones in directing them toward treatment. Those efforts are sometimes not even attempted or, if attempted, are ineffective. It is often left to the legal, medical, or mental health systems to get people into treatment. Those systems are quite imperfect. In contrast, family and friends are some of the most powerful forces in people's lives, and they can sometimes have far more effective (and benign) influence in getting people into treatment.

What stops most people who want to help is not knowing how to begin to talk to a troubled person. It's awkward. The person's responses can be sharp and rejecting. And so many areas are unfamiliar—where to turn for help, how to access resources that are already in place, how to learn about mental illness and its treatment, how to use legal mechanisms that can help people get treatment, how to link up with organizations that can help guide and support the process. Most people know how to help a friend who has discovered a lump in her breast. *Call your doctor right now and get in for an exam and mammogram!* In contrast, very few people know how to approach a friend or relative with an emotional problem. In this book, you will learn why it is vital to get beyond that awkwardness and be able to start the conversation. To say, *Can we talk?*

I know there are many reasons why you have avoided this conversation or had difficulties with it, and the chapters that follow examine those reasons. But know right now that there is no shame in needing mental health care.

State-of-the-art treatment for these kinds of problems can work very well, and people do *not* have to be "crazy" to avail themselves of such effective help. Many of us take comfort in finding that highly successful celebrities we admire have real-life problems, too. Actress Catherine Zeta-Jones has admitted publicly that she has bipolar disorder, and Congressman Patrick Kennedy and Carrie Fisher (Princess Leia from the *Star Wars* movies) have been frank about their bipolar disorder and substance abuse problems. One of the most famous psychotherapists in the nation today, Marsha Linehan, has admitted her own incredibly severe history of mental illness, which inspired her to develop pioneering and highly successful therapy techniques. Singer Bruce Springsteen, beloved by fans around the world, has been forthcoming about his clinical depression and how therapy helped him.

I became a psychiatrist because I always found psychological pain to be one of the most *human* forms of suffering. Physical pain is something that we closely share with our animal brethren. But depression, paranoia, anxiety, irrational obsessive thoughts, and other symptoms of mental distress are all particularly, if not uniquely, human. As a medical student, I discovered that ministering to this kind of suffering gave me a real sense of what it means to be a physician. Psychiatry allowed me to explore the deepest interior of others. I came to understand what Marcel Proust once eloquently wrote: "The only true voyage of discovery would not be to visit strange lands, but to behold the universe through the eyes of another."

The other reason I went into psychiatry was my belief in the power of words. Words are among the *most powerful* ways that human beings can influence the world, especially each other. After all, in the Bible, speaking is the very tool with which God creates the entire universe: "And God *said*, let there be light!" I originally went to Johns Hopkins Hospital to train in internal medicine. In the middle of the first year, I was fed up with having so little time to spend with my patients. It seemed like I was constantly tracking down the results of lab tests and imaging studies. I was not particularly good with my hands either, so procedures like starting IVs—putting instruments into delicate tissues— were not easy for me. It was all very interesting, but not very satisfying. One night after being on call, I was walking in downtown Baltimore when I came across an unconscious homeless person lying on a steam grate. He was being ignored by everyone else on the sidewalk, and it was tempting to pass him by. I couldn't. I was able to arouse him and immediately saw that he was mentally ill. I called an ambulance and he was taken to a hospital down the street. Something inside me clicked during that act of reaching out. The next day I made an appointment to see Dr. Phillip Slavney, the director of residency training in the psychiatry department at Johns Hopkins, to find out more about the psychiatry residency. I lamented that I felt I wasn't very good with scalpels and such. What he said changed my life: "Well, you know, in psychiatry *words are our scalpels." That* made sense to me. Words were something I felt competent wielding; their power was something I had experienced, both at the giving and receiving ends. I knew words could create, and destroy. Right there, on the spot, I asked if I could transfer over to the psychiatry residency program the next year. And I did.

Words that can help people change became my professional craft. In this book, I want to share words that can help you help others. Speaking in ways that express concern, that do not shame, and that provide direction to help might allow you to reach the goal of this book: a professional evaluation for the person of concern in your life. Your words may, at times, need to be firm—even tough. Sometimes you may need to go beyond speaking with the particular person in trouble, speaking also with his or her family members, friends, doctors, clergy, and maybe even civil authorities. Sometimes, you may have to do more than talk—you may have to take firm actions.

Telling other adults what to do is far more difficult than guiding and steering children. Thus, this book focuses specifically on approaching troubled adults, where the challenge is the greatest. That other adult may be your grown child; in fact, it is very likely that you picked up this book because you are struggling with approaching your older adolescent or adult child. But most of the following ideas can apply as well to friends, a spouse, even coworkers.

My method here is not to explore individual psychiatric conditions in detail. Many excellent books and websites are already available that describe nearly every psychiatric disorder (and I have provided many references in the resources section on pages 241–256). Nor is this book about the specifics of treatments and the many different methods for treating mental health problems. You don't need to know the diagnostic term for what afflicts your person of concern; you don't need to know if you should get a book on depression, or addiction, or anxiety, or psychosis. You just need to know: "This person needs more professional help than I can give."

This book is divided into two sections. The first four chapters provide the background to help you understand why you might have come to need a book like this. These chapters help you focus on your primary goal: getting the troubled person to seek a professional psychiatric evaluation. The last six chapters are a step-by-step practical guide to accomplishing that goal. If you are in a hurry to use the "how-to" portion of this book, you can go directly to chapter 5 and come back later to the first section.

- Chapter 1 helps you to see when it's time for professional evaluation—when things have become too serious for your efforts alone, and a threshold has been crossed. Your reluctance to get involved is squarely addressed, and you are encouraged to overcome your own natural resistance.

- Chapter 2 demonstrates that mental problems are widespread, and it discusses the consequences of untreated mental disorders.

- Chapter 3 reviews many possible reasons why the troubled-other hasn't sought treatment on his or her own—hence your need to help.

- Chapter 4 clarifies the core goal of this book: the initial professional evaluation of the troubled person. I review what happens in the mental health evaluation, some of the available treatments, and who best to do the evaluation. I will also give you tips about how to find an appropriate professional.

- Chapter 5 helps you consider the timing—good times to approach the troubled-other, and times you want to avoid. Also, the chapter helps you think about the right place.

- Chapter 6 helps you with the opening pitch, that is, how to begin to talk about the problem one-on-one. The chapter suggests effective communication strategies that have a chance of "getting to *yes.*"

- Chapter 7 is useful if the private communications of chapter 6 are ineffective. You are encouraged to think of allies who might join you in the effort and how to mobilize their influence.

- Chapter 8 steps up the pressure further, moving from talk to action, spelling out approaches to "therapeutic coercion." I will show you how to use the power inherent in your relationship to channel the person toward that all-important initial evaluation. Although very powerful, these measures have the potential for conflict, and you may be tempted to avoid them. Yet, it is failure to engage the troubled-other at this level that often accounts for failure to get that professional evaluation, which might open the door to proper treatment. I will fortify your resolve and skill in using these more challenging approaches, should they be necessary.

- Chapter 9 is for situations that are acute and dangerous, where the softball approaches of the previous chapters are either ineffective or too slow. Here you will learn how to utilize the systems society has in place for involuntary evaluation of acutely mentally ill people. This chapter also considers your personal safety and the safety of children.

- Chapter 10 gives tips about what to do *after* the goal of evaluation is reached. If you can attend the evaluation, this chapter suggests how to most effectively use your presence, how to connect and stay connected with the care provider, and how to support the ongoing treatment of your person of concern. It raises the consideration of professional help for you, should you need it. This chapter also addresses the possibility that, in spite of everything you have tried, you may still have an unexamined or untreated person with continuing psychiatric symptoms on your hands. What then?

- The appendix summarizes the book's recommended process and methods for convincing a loved one to get help, as well as offering further steps to take should you run into resistance. You can use this list as a handy reference guide while putting the different suggestions from this book into practice.

- The resources sections list sources for further information and ways to find professional help.

I encourage you to read this book from beginning to end, and then return to the chapters that are relevant as you progress in your efforts to help your friend or loved one. It is possible that you are facing a very urgent situation in which the person you are trying to help is in danger, either because of the threat of suicide or violent behavior. There may not be time to read this entire book right now. Chapter 6 offers suggestions for approaching the subject of suicide with your loved one and resources for additional support. Chapter 9 will help you get rapidly acquainted with how to mobilize the authorities to assist in a suicidal or violent situation. You can also call the National Suicide Prevention Lifeline at 1-800-273-TALK or visit www.suicidepreventionlifeline.org for more information.

Numerous studies have confirmed my own clinical observations: compared to other health problems, psychiatric problems can cause some of the worst suffering; and not just to those people who have a mental illness, but to those people who live and work with the mentally ill. This book will offer solutions to that suffering. *You Need Help!* includes stories of real, suffering people and those who struggle to help them. You will read examples of conversations you can initiate with your loved one, friend, or colleague. My hope is that reading this book will help you bring well-being and sanity to the life of the troubled person and to your own life as well. This book will give you hope and comfort that *something* can be done and that *you* can be instrumental in bringing about positive change.

What a person with a mental disorder really needs is *you*. Why you? Because you have a *relationship* with this person. You care about him or her. Your caring may have many faces: you may love him, you may have to raise children together, you may have to work together, you may share a loyalty that comes from experience or blood, you may have known each other for years, you may have great respect for him, he may have helped you in the past, you may have promised another person to care for him. Whatever the reason, enough caring exists for you to have picked up this book. That means that the other person cares about you in return—cares about your opinions, your feelings, and your ideas. Maybe the other's ability to experience that caring is dimmed by the mental problem itself. But, somewhere, behind the symptoms, an ember of a relationship with you still glows—an ember of warmth you can reach.

Hippocrates, the ancient Greek father of medicine, wrote, "Sometimes doing nothing is the best remedy." You've tried that remedy, and it has failed. You are now more than ready to access other remedies that are available in our time, more than two thousand years later. Turn the page. You can start learning how, right now.

1

Should You Get Involved?

"If I cannot do great things,
I will do small things in a great way."
— MOTHER TERESA

You are reading this book because someone you care about has *changed* in a way that concerns you—and is getting worse. This is a person with whom you have a close relationship—family member, friend, or coworker—someone you have known since long before the problem began. Now, on a regular basis, you are witnessing behaviors that seem out of character, and you are worried.

Should you ignore what you see and hear? Laugh it off? Deliver a pep talk? Or have things reached the point where your support alone would be insufficient? Perhaps you're beginning to sense that more substantial help is needed— help from a mental health professional. Yet, you're not sure if your hunch is correct or, even if it is, whether you should interfere. You may be wondering, *Why am I thinking about getting involved at all? Can't (my spouse, son, daughter, friend, colleague) seek mental health treatment without my assistance?* You are in an uncomfortable position, and you may be tempted to play the waiting game. How *do* you know if you should get involved? The first step is recognizing when help *is* needed. Lonnie's friends wish they had.

• LONNIE •

Lonnie, a professional basketball player, had experienced a difficult childhood. His father had abandoned the family when Lonnie was five, and he was raised by a single mother in a poor inner-city neighborhood. She took great pains to protect him from the allure of gangs, scraping together the funds to enroll him in an after-school basketball league. He showed incredible natural talent and, with good coaching, Lonnie excelled. His success on the basketball court influenced him in the classroom and his grades improved. Eventually, he earned a basketball scholarship at a major southern university. After graduation, he was drafted into the NBA.

As happy as he was to be playing basketball for a living, Lonnie was not one of the stars on his team. Over time, he became jealous of the players who garnered the attention of the media and fans. At the same time, he was using cocaine and alcohol with increasing frequency. To those who knew him, he began to appear increasingly negative. Eventually, he began talking about not wanting to live. Some of his teammates ridiculed him for talking like this. His friends knew this was out of character but couldn't believe it was serious. After all, wasn't he making a lot of money, and at a "dream" job?

Lonnie began sleeping for twelve hours a day, missing practices, and becoming more temperamental. His friends were concerned, but figured, "It goes with the territory" of professional sports. When Lonnie mentioned that he wanted to kill himself, his friend thought he was "just being dramatic."

One morning, Lonnie was found unconscious in a hotel room by a teammate who had come by to get him for breakfast. He had taken an overdose of a girlfriend's cocaine. That's when I met him, in the ER, where an ambulance had brought him. In addition to evaluating him, I spent time with his distressed friends, who were shocked and feeling guilty that they hadn't taken him seriously.

The Difference Between Ordinary and Serious Problems

In the United States today, many adults have slightly elevated blood pressure. Most of these folks don't need medication; a few changes in diet and lifestyle are sufficient to get their numbers down to a healthy range. Similarly, not every troubled person needs psychotherapy or medication. Psychiatrists and other mental health care providers recommend good mental health habits and encourage preventive measures—relaxation techniques, stress reduction techniques, meditation, exercise—all the things you read about in consumer magazines. Compared to psychotherapy or medication, these are considered "first aid" rather than "treatment." Psychotherapy and medication are powerful measures, and both have side effects. Treatment providers need to be certain that the gains outweigh the risks, and to obey the primary ethical mission of the Hippocratic Oath: "Above all else, do no harm."

The majority of problems with thoughts, feelings, and behaviors are run-of-the-mill, and most people can "work it out" themselves. We don't need professional mental health experts for our common stresses and distresses. A good friend, someone who's a good listener, maybe even an attentive hair stylist, is enough.

What is the difference, then, between the everyday troubles we all face and "clinically significant" problems that can benefit enormously from modern treatment techniques? And how do you recognize the difference?

It's one thing to be down in the dumps—anxious about whether you can pay the bills, worried about your child's school performance, short-tempered with your kids, or sad that so many of your friends are dying (common among the elderly). It's altogether different, however, if you are so distressed or out of control that *your functioning begins to shut down*, or *you are hurting those around you*, or *you are destroying your relationships by slow degrees*.

What Is "Normal"?

Callers to my radio show would sometimes urge me to give an answer to a popular question: "What is normal anyway?" My answer was often, "Normal is just somebody you don't know very well!" When the laughing was over, I'd give Sigmund Freud's definition of normal: "The ability to love and work effectively." This is so clear and sensible it is still quoted by psychiatrists, to each other and to our patients. Let this be your guide: when things start to go significantly haywire in the world of love and work (and self-coping measures don't cut it), it's time to take advantage of some expertise. It's time to "get some help!"

When Is It Time to Get Professional Help?

There are many signs that a threshold has been crossed: You can't eat or sleep adequately. You are so exhausted you can't get up in the morning. You are unable to concentrate and start making mistakes at work. You are angry all the time and so irritating to others that you are repeatedly rejected. You can't form an enduring attachment. Your temper outbursts are so bad you are fired from your job, or your spouse leaves you. As bad as it looks to the concerned onlooker, for the troubled person experiencing these problems, the need for professional help may not be obvious. That's why it often takes the concern of a friend, relative, or colleague to start the conversation.

The American Psychiatric Association (APA) has a list of ten warning signs that indicate the need for evaluation by someone with expertise in the mind and brain. Any *one* of them is enough to raise a flag that help might be needed:

1. Marked personality change
2. Inability to cope with problems and daily activities
3. Strange or grandiose ideas
4. Excessive anxieties
5. Prolonged depression and apathy
6. Marked changes in eating or sleeping patterns
7. Talking or even thinking about suicide
8. Extreme moods—highs and lows
9. Abuse of alcohol or drugs
10. Excessive anger, hostility, or violent behavior

The U.S. Department of Health and Human Services has published its own list of nine warning signs, which partially overlap the APA's. The list can be found on the website www.samhsa.gov/economy, under Getting Through Tough Economic Times:

1. Persistent sadness/crying
2. Excessive anxiety

3. Lack of sleep/constant fatigue

4. Excessive irritability/anger

5. Increased drinking

6. Illicit drug use, including misuse of medications

7. Difficulty paying attention or staying focused

8. Apathy—not caring about things that are usually important

9. Not being able to function as well at work, school, or home

Some Signs That Help Is Needed

Here is my own personal list, with real-life examples, of some basic signs that someone needs to "get help." What follows isn't intended to be a complete list—when a mother talks about wanting to kill her children, you don't need a mental health professional to point out that such a person is in need of *urgent* help. It is a list of the most common (yet serious) signals and circumstances that indicate mental health problems, and any one of them should cause you to take notice. Examples are grouped within categories, based on the nature of the problems. (Note: An asterisk (*) indicates that a certain behavior is more commonly seen in that gender.)

1. Making others suffer or feel scared:

- Behavior that repeatedly scares you (you fear for his* safety, your safety, or someone else's safety).

- A significant temper problem that is consistently frightening or intimidating to others, and he* is not aware that his temper is having that effect on others.

2. Problems taking care of or regulating one's self:

- She stops taking care of her basic hygiene—bathing, changing clothes, brushing teeth, etc.

- A change in sleep, appetite, or energy that has lasted at least two weeks.

- She starts doing things that seem reckless and are "just not like her"—such as drinking too much, going on shopping sprees and making impulsive purchases, going on frivolous trips, taking on an excessive number of projects, or needing less sleep (zero to four hours/night) without being tired the next day.

- She* keeps going to medical doctors for physical complaints and is repeatedly told that there are no significant physical findings, but continues to "doctor-shop," relentlessly searching for physical explanations for bodily complaints.

- She* tries to lose weight and can't stop dieting. Fear of being fat (despite being a fairly normal weight or even being slightly underweight) is dominating her thoughts and conversations.

- Day and night are reversed and he is sleeping most of the day and awake most of the night.

- He has repeatedly behaved in embarrassing or mean ways when drinking. Sometimes he doesn't remember behaving in these ways. You or others have mentioned to him that he might do well to cut back. He did, for a while, but that effort was short-lived, and the drinking is again frequent and disturbing to others.

- She* has deliberately cut or hurt herself, or tried to take her life.

3. Problems with thinking:

- He is making more mistakes than usual, forgetting important things, misplacing possessions, making unusual messes of the house or office. Be especially concerned if forgetfulness causes potentially dangerous situations (leaving the stove on, letting the bathtub overflow, etc.).

- She starts to talk about things that are obviously not true—saying she* is fat when she is really thin, thinking her walls and phones are bugged, believing there is some conspiracy against her, thinking she is dreadfully sick when there is little or no evidence of it, etc.

- He is increasingly confused and disoriented, and can't seem to think straight.

- She is seeing or hearing things that nobody else does.

- She* can't remember buying certain clothes in her closet, believes strangers call her by a different name (that she doesn't recognize), or can't remember what she did or where she was for hours at a stretch.

4. Intense feelings:

- She* is having anxieties that make it difficult for her to leave the house, or she fears "going crazy" or having a heart attack (often, under these circumstances, people will make multiple trips to the emergency room, and they will usually leave with a surprisingly good bill of physical health after the panic attack subsides).

- He has repeating and intrusive thoughts or rituals that he knows are irrational, but can't seem to control, often thinking thoughts or doing things until "it feels right to stop."

- He talks or writes about wanting to die, or he repeatedly wishes natural causes would "just take me."
- She believes that she should be punished for terrible things she has done (they might not seem so terrible to you). These things may have never bothered her this much before.

5. Problems relating or socializing:

- She has withdrawn from the things she used to do and from people she used to enjoy.
- He can't sustain significant social relationships, starts losing friends, becomes increasingly isolated, and can't initiate sustained intimate relationships.
- He* is having problems functioning sexually, or desiring sex, or is having highly unusual and risky sexual fantasies. Or he is engaged in sexual behaviors that are risky or hurtful to his partner.

6. Problems working:

- She can't seem to hold or get a job, especially if she has shown early promise by doing well in school; or she had a good work record for a while, but it suddenly goes awry.
- He used to be an adequate or better student, but his grades have been declining now for more than a semester. He is neglecting assignments, something he hasn't done before. He is not working at the same level as he used to and seems not to notice or care about this decline.

7. Traumatic life events:

- She* was sexually or physically abused as a child.

- He was exposed to some kind of accident or other event in which he believed his life was ending. Since then, he is having problems with a variety of functions such as concentrating and sleeping, and is experiencing frequent and inappropriate anxiety.

- She has experienced the death of a child or the loss of a family member by suicide.

- He or she has just experienced a marital separation or divorce or breakup of a longstanding, significant personal relationship.

As previously stated, these lists are not exhaustive. Moreover, these are *possible* warning signs of mental health problems. These might also be symptoms of physical illnesses—hormonal problems, cancers, metabolic problems, and so on. And even if it is determined that there is a mental health issue, the evaluation may not lead to treatment; sometimes the right approach is "wait and see." At the very least, however, a relationship needs to be established with a mental health professional so that if problems worsen access to help is in place. (Making the *second* call for help is much easier than the first.)

Problems with Thoughts, Feelings, or Behaviors

As you look over the preceding lists, it is helpful to think about the ways that things can go wrong as falling into one of three categories: problems of *thoughts*, *feelings*, or *behaviors*.

In general, treatment approaches to problems in each of these three areas are somewhat different, as we now understand that different neurological and chemical systems in the brain are relevant for thoughts, for feelings, and for behaviors. Similarly, life experience can influence these three domains in different ways.

You've Changed

One thing clinicians look for is "change from baseline." We all have a baseline—a "business as usual" way of behaving, feeling, and living. Healthy people are surprisingly consistent in this way. So, when behavior deviates markedly from a long-established pattern, it should be considered a potential warning sign. This kind of change in a person's behavior is a critical sign of a possible psychiatric disorder.

An example of change from baseline that made headlines is the case of Lisa Nowak, the astronaut who suddenly deviated from leading an accomplished life that included a remarkably successful career in the astronaut corps. She began to behave in a way that was out of step with social norms and very unlike her "baseline" behavior. Eventually, armed with a variety of paraphernalia, she drove nine hundred miles to confront her rival in a love triangle, threatening kidnapping and mayhem. In clinical terms, her actions represented a "deviation from a prior, established baseline." Her behavior left no doubt in anyone's mind: *This woman needs help!*

More on Traumatic Life Events

Traumatic life events refer to having been through an experience that can predispose a person to mental health issues. A history of being physically or verbally abused as a child, witnessing repeated violence to others in a childhood household, the breakup of a major long-term relationship (especially a marriage), the death of a child and/or suicide of a loved one, or a near-death experience are some of the most wounding things that can happen to anyone. No one gets through these events without significant emotional pain, embarrassment, or shame. These experiences can inflict scars on the psyche that critically alter the rest of one's life.

When such events are part of one's biography, psychiatric evaluation can be helpful even if there is *not* a current problem with thoughts, feelings, or behaviors. Why? It's very likely that there will be significant problems in these areas eventually. Effects are likely to eventually show up in relationships with one's children, coworkers, or significant others. They may drive a person to overwork, to be sexually compulsive, to be imperious with coworkers, or to demonstrate other problematic behaviors. The effects of traumatic experiences can manifest in a wide variety of dysfunctional behaviors or emotions, even if the traumatized person might *feel* that the memories are no longer specifically painful. Those experiences can still have a psychological legacy. Evaluation based on this kind of history *alone* offers an opportunity for a mental health professional to provide what is called "secondary prevention"—addressing a problem early to prevent it from leading to more hurtful consequences. If the evaluation doesn't reveal a current problem, it does create a connection with a health care professional— an open door that will be easier to walk through should symptoms emerge later. Think of it this way: if you had been in a burning building and inhaled smoke, you would get checked out by a doctor. It may turn out that no damage has been done. On the other hand, your lungs may have been scorched, which could lead to pulmonary problems down the road. Your doctor now knows you and can help anticipate and even prevent consequences.

When a marriage or a similar long-term committed relationship fails, I believe it is critical to debrief with an expert.

Sometimes when a significant relationship breaks up, people see themselves as more disturbed and "messed up" than they really are, and they need to be brought back to a more realistic view of themselves. Alternatively, people can dismiss the whole thing as the fault of an aberrant mate who is "the crazy one." It can be helpful to take an unflinching look at the emotional problems that you may have brought to the relationship, before possibly infecting your next relationship with those same problems. Either way, *all* individuals who experience the end of a significant committed relationship owe it to themselves, and to their future mates, to get some kind of expert evaluation, even if only a few sessions. This is *not* because they have an illness or disease or major clinical problem. They simply need to process what has happened in order to get back their sense of self, and to look at parts of themselves they may not have been able or willing to see. There is a principle well known to mental health professionals: a crisis often offers a valuable opportunity for critical self-examination. Even the stingiest insurance companies understand this. I have yet to see managed care reviewers deny coverage for psychiatric treatment (most commonly, talk therapy) of someone whose marriage is breaking up.

Should I Get Involved? The Moral Dilemma

Even if you've identified signs that your friend or loved one needs treatment or an evaluation by a mental health professional, you may not be sure you should intervene. You may question whether it's the right thing to do. Your internal struggle is not surprising. We live in a society that prizes individuality, individual rights, free speech, and self-determination. As a culture, we are highly suspicious of anyone who wants us to curb our behavior in any way, except when we cross the threshold of hurting others or ourselves.

The balance between tolerating misbehavior and emotional malfunctioning on one hand, and the preservation of personal liberty and civil rights on the other hand, is a delicate one. Throughout the latter part of the twentieth century, civil rights have largely outweighed other considerations. This was the ethical argument behind ending forced institutionalization of the mentally ill, beginning in 1955, which ultimately led to the now 2.2 million Americans with untreated severe mental illness, of whom about 150,000 are homeless on any given day.

What gives anyone the right to get involved in another person's most personal business, his mental life, that most private of private realms? Are there legitimate, compassionate reasons to try and persuade someone we care about to go into treatment? There are, indeed, a few.

Consider this: If your mother was losing her memory and intellectual functioning, was leaving the stove on, letting the bathtub overflow, or wandering into the snow in her nightgown, would you hesitate to bring her to the doctor and secure her living environment? Probably not. You wouldn't speak about her eccentricity, her right to be different, and her freedom to do as she pleases. You would be crying out for help, and getting her to an expert as soon as possible. Perhaps you would justify this because she is "sick" and "in danger." Yet the idea of being "sick and in danger" is something that applies to a wide variety of mental health problems, not just dementia (senility).

When you are on the fence about getting involved in another's personal life, a review of the potential consequences of untreated mental illness may prove to be the tipping point. These consequences include

- physical danger to self or others—physical violence, suicide, neglect of other health problems
- emotional harm to children—neglect, abuse, shaming, and emotional torment
- emotional abuse to partners or spouses
- financial problems
- accidents

Compassion Is a Moral Starting Point

It is heartbreaking to see another human being suffer in any way. Physical pain is something that we share with our animal brethren. But depression, paranoia, anxiety, irrational obsessive thoughts, and other symptoms of mental illness are uniquely human.

Our basic human empathy for the emotional pain of others causes us to respond with compassion. We want to *do* something to see our loved ones healed and their sufferings soothed. Why then, as a caring family member, friend, or colleague are we reluctant to suggest psychiatric help, let alone force it? Is it because we feel it's impolite? Is it because we are reluctant to meddle? Because we are afraid our friend will feel insulted, or become angry?

When someone you care about is in obvious emotional pain, giving a nudge toward a professional assessment or treatment is not meddling, it is *caring*. It is an expression of compassion. It is consistent with religious traditions to "Love thy neighbor as thyself."

In a pamphlet published by Hazelden in 1993 called *When Someone You Care about Abuses Drugs and Alcohol,* the author talks poignantly about the obstacles faced when trying to help a loved one who is abusing alcohol and drugs. I find the situation applies equally well to *all* mental health problems:

> Why, when we have friends whose drinking behavior or drug use disturbs us, do we talk *about* them instead of directly *to* them? Is it because we are afraid? What are we afraid of? That our friends will become angry at us, will feel insulted and maybe even retaliate by telling us what they don't like about us? That we will not be considered *nice*? That it's rude and tactless to speak up when we are concerned about someone's behavior? That if we were a real friend, we would overlook almost anything? That our statement will be interpreted as criticism, and our friend will be hurt or react with resentment? All these fears come from a sense of propriety that is appropriate in certain situations. But if we're dealing with a friend who has a drinking or drug problem [or other psychiatric problem], silence can be deadly. Because when people who drink or use drugs are not held accountable for or made aware of their behavior, they may believe they're still okay and can get away with using a little longer.

Indeed, intervening on another's behalf with compassion is what medical ethicists call *beneficence*: doing something for the relief of another, rather than for ourselves. To approach another with beneficence requires three things. First, it requires the ability to see that someone is in distress. Second, it requires a clear understanding of your needs and the other person's needs, so as to not confuse the two. Third, you need to know your limitations and when to call in additional help from an expert.

This third point is worth thinking about more closely. It is natural to try to talk with someone who is distressed, to give support, even to provide some advice. You don't have to be a bartender, hairdresser, or cab driver to have played that role. As a psychiatrist, I think about this kind of compassionate support as "first aid." But, when the bleeding starts—it's time to get the experts!

If you sense the problem is out of your league or you feel helpless in the face of the person's suffering, the compassionate—the *ethical*—thing to do is to convince that person to see a mental health professional.

Paternalism Is a Good Thing,
If It Can Restore Autonomy

The word "paternalism" is out of fashion today. For young people, it conjures up images of controlling, authoritarian parents. For feminists, it calls to mind male-dominated patriarchy. Yet the concept of paternalism is one half of a pair of time-honored ethical concepts, the other half of which is "autonomy."

"Paternalism" is a word derived from the role a parent naturally has toward a child: caretaking, stewardship, and empowerment. What does paternalism hope to empower? One and one thing *only*—autonomy. "Autonomy" means an individual can choose his or her own actions. It is based on the assumption that the person is capable of making clear and rational decisions.

Medical ethicists have accepted the idea that sometimes, particularly when people are sick, the capacity to make rational decisions is diminished, even if only temporarily.

Then, the ability to act autonomously is lowered. In this circumstance, it is ethical and appropriate to exercise stewardship over the diminished person's welfare, according to the degree to which the person is impaired. This "taking charge" approach, helping do what needs to be done, taking the lead in getting help and making an intervention, is what we mean by "medical paternalism." Paternalism and autonomy are a seesaw in the arena of caring for sick people—when one is up, the other is down. For example, when a person arrives in the emergency room unconscious, it is ethically permissible to start medical interventions. As he recovers, awakens, and gradually gets his wits about him, more of his consent is sought with each improvement in mental clarity.

Of all things that can go wrong in the human body, a malfunctioning mind (sometimes due to a malfunctioning brain) has the greatest implications for a person's autonomy. As described later, in chapter 3, many psychiatric conditions can lead to states of reduced insight into one's self (like mania), produce a profound inability to relate to one's surroundings (like catatonia or delirium), or create irrational states of mind (like obsessive-compulsive disorder). So, by their nature, mental or emotional problems can diminish a person's autonomy. This invites (some ethicists might say *requires*) a paternalistic response on the part of those who are duty-bound, whether by profession or by the bonds of love and caring, to help. That means leading the way rather than watching, waiting, and hoping for the best.

You Are Not Being Selfish

Your desire to help someone get psychiatric treatment may also be due to your own needs, especially if you are feeling hurt, burdened, worried, or threatened by the person. There is absolutely no shame in wanting some relief for yourself. Living with someone who has a mental illness or some kind of emotional disturbance can be challenging. Family members can suffer innumerable consequences because of a loved one's mental illness, including violence in a small number of cases. Life with a person who is de-pressed can be depressing, and quite frustrating. Emotions, both positive and negative, can become "infectious."

It can be hard to resist participating in the problem. Ron's story illustrates how easily one can be drafted into another's illness.

• RON •

For the last five years, Ron has been terrified of being contaminated by bacteria. He insists that his wife wipe off the bottoms of her shoes whenever she enters the house, take out the trash for him (he is too scared to touch it) five times a day, and flush the toilet for him. When the phone rings, Ron uses a tissue to pick up the receiver. He becomes incensed if his wife moves the box of tissues that he keeps by the phone. If she doesn't comply with these and the many other demands he makes to keep him from "contamination," he yells at her, insists that she doesn't care about him, even cries. She has found it easier to just give in and "keep the peace."

Sometimes, without meaning to, you become part of the problem and suffer the consequences of another's mental illness, even inadvertently supporting or enabling it. This is a remarkably common scenario. I have been shocked to see how long some families tolerate extreme behaviors without even *suggesting* the troubled person get help. Withdrawal, anger, paranoia, depression, and other typical psychiatric symptoms rapidly take a heavy toll on others, far more so than symptoms of medical illnesses like fever, coughing, vomiting, or pain. What's more, psychiatric problems are often more chronic and enduring. They are wearing and corrosive to relationships, especially because (for reasons that will be discussed in chapter 3) they often take longer to get the attention they need compared to other medical problems. Let's face it: if someone is vomiting for two days, it's very likely that the doctor will be called. Depression can last months, even years, before a doctor might be called.

If *you* are in distress, know that it is quite common, appropriate, and expected to want to help someone for your *own* needs. Taking care of yourself is a first step in the process of helping another. If you have ever travelled by air, you are familiar with the flight attendants' instructions about the oxygen masks. What do you do if you are traveling with a small child? Do you put the mask on yourself or the child first? It is interesting how many veteran flyers answer this question incorrectly. The correct answer is that you put on *your* mask first before helping the child. This is because you need to take care of your own oxygen supply before you can help another who is less capable.

It may even be necessary for the helper to get some treatment of her own, which may include support for dealing with the person with mental health problems. Such counseling not only may help you keep your own head above water but also may show how you have unwittingly become part of the problem. You may see that you are enabling the problem by your need to "keep the peace." Perhaps the problem has triggered a psychiatric condition in you that needs treatment, such as depression or anxiety disorder. Getting treatment for yourself, or other forms of support, is covered in coming chapters.

Not Every Problem Needs a Psychiatrist

Just as psychiatry has, at times, oversold itself, people sometimes overvalue psychiatry and related mental health professions. It is at least optimistic, maybe unrealistic, to think that every human problem can be solved by talking, taking medication, or some kind of professional behavioral plan. The famous psychiatrist Karl Menninger proposed early in the twentieth century to reform every prisoner with psychiatric treatment. There has always been a lurking hope that ultimately the science of the human mind can correct all wrongs, erase all evil inclinations, and stop all destructive or selfish behaviors. We are far from that horizon. Might the science of human psychology and the brain help in any particular situation? I maintain simply, "It can't hurt to ask." In other words, getting an evaluation to see *if* the troubling problems *might* be amenable to state-of-the-art treatment is worth it. A good, honest, competent professional (and, really, most are) will be able to say if you are in the wrong place, if the concepts and skills of a mental health professional are not applicable. A worldly and thoughtful professional might have suggestions for a *better* route: maybe a lawyer, an accountant, a clergyperson, or maybe an investment consultant, a career counselor, or a neurosurgeon. The point is *you* do not have to decide if psychiatric treatment is the right way to go. If the problem involves thoughts, feelings, or behaviors, getting the opinion of a psychiatric expert as to whether this is the right path could be the start of treatment, or the end of this particular line and the opening of a new idea.

• • •

In this chapter, you learned the most common ways things can go haywire in a person's mental life, under what circumstances a psychiatrist or other mental health professional can be helpful, and that intervening is a morally sound move. Next, I'll give you basic information on mental health problems so that you can be a more fully informed guide in your efforts to help the troubled other.

2

A Closer Look at Mental Health Problems

"Diseases of the soul are more dangerous and more numerous than those of the body."

— CICERO

It's likely that you want to help someone in your life in emotional or mental trouble because some tipping point has occurred, and you are no longer willing to be an observer of the problem—you want to find a solution. Your reasons for feeling this way can be myriad. The pain that's evident in your friend may move you. Or maybe the pain that *you* are experiencing—caused by your friend's behavior—has motivated you to seek a course of action. It could also be the disruption you see in the lives of those closest to him, or the chaos he is causing in his social and professional environment. Whatever the reason, you are ready to do something.

What's Going On?

Last night, your adult daughter was at your house for dinner, as she always is on Tuesdays. But she was short-tempered and rude. You've watched as over the last few months she has become more and more irritable. Lately, she arrives with a bottle of wine and drinks most of it before dinner is served. The next day, when she calls to thank you for dinner, she appears to have forgotten how rude she was, and never apologizes. This morning she didn't call. Now you and your husband are worried that your daughter is abusing alcohol. You've tried to talk to her about her drinking, but she explodes. Now you're afraid to say anything because her temper is close to the boiling point.

A close friend of yours is acting strangely. You and she have a long-standing lunch date every other Tuesday, but lately she's been canceling at the last minute. When you call her at the office, the receptionist tells you that she's not in. You ran into her husband at the grocery store and he told you that she hasn't been sleeping well and she's been missing days at work. You don't know whether she has lost interest in your friendship, whether she's having an affair, or whether she's having emotional problems and needs help.

Your brother called and suggested you keep your living room curtains closed because "they might be watching." "Who is watching?" you ask him. "The people in the red cars; I saw three of them on my way home today, and they all had license plates beginning with the number three. I think they're watching people who have three kids, like you." This conversation only adds to the worries you have had about him, like noticing that he isn't changing his clothes very much and it seems to be a long time since he took a shower. At the last family dinner with your parents, he came late, seemed very uncomfortable, and left abruptly.

Your mother has been piling up magazines and newspapers for years. She genuinely intends to read them, but she now has thousands stacked in piles all over the main rooms of the house and in spare bedrooms; *thirty years of paper!*

There are "paths" between the piles, but they are getting more and more narrow. The place is a fire hazard. Your attempts to convince her that she doesn't really need to save these things (especially now, in the Internet age), and that she'll never read them, have been fruitless. You tell her that she may have some kind of psychological problem, but she thinks it is *you* who has the problem if you can't understand why these things are so precious to her, so vital, so important to keep.

What do you say to these people? Do they see that they are behaving unusually, or have changed? Should you say anything? Don't they seem like they need some kind of professional help? Is there a way to tell them that? What if they get upset at that advice or refuse?

Before you can understand *how* to help, it's beneficial to begin by looking at the range of emotional and mental problems people can struggle with, as well as the ramifications of untreated mental illness. This information will be instructive as you consider why the person you're worried about may be avoiding seeking professional help.

What Exactly Are *Mental* Problems?

There are three major expressions of mental life: *thoughts*, *feelings*, and *behaviors*. You can think of these as the three legs of a stool. A problem or weakening in any one (or more) of these supports will throw off the stool's balance. In the brain—the seat of mental life—problems with thoughts, feelings, or behaviors can lead to suffering and problems functioning. And as you have already observed, those problems can also affect those whose lives intersect the life of the troubled person.

Problems in mental health come in many forms. Interestingly (and surprising to the population at large), the most common manifestations are *not* the sort that make splashy news headlines. They are far less dramatic. Examples include

- anxiety that inhibits the ability to travel
- depression that limits productivity and prevents a promotion at work
- temper outbursts that scare and intimidate family members, and alienate friends
- compulsiveness that slows one's academic studies so that it's impossible to keep up with class
- drinking that has deteriorated the trust and caring in a close relationship
- intrusive thoughts that interfere with sleep at night
- obsessive health concerns that result in numerous visits to the doctor and unnecessary medical testing

These are all common consequences from mental problems that can result from recognized conditions. The good news is these conditions benefit from well-established treatments. Yes, there are more exotic mental health problems that involve hallucinations and delusions, paranoia, threatening behavior, lost memories, enormous energy, catatonic withdrawal, lewd speech, and incoherent expression. Though not as common, one of these disorders may well be affecting your loved one. Whether the condition is a common mental health issue, or a more severe and less-common one, this book can help you in your goal of getting the troubled person to accept professional help. And that is always the first step in addressing any health problem, mental or physical.

Four Perspectives

In their book *The Perspectives of Psychiatry*,[1] Paul McHugh and Phillip Slavney group mental health problems into four basic categories:

- *Disease:* Problems best understood as "diseases" result from distinct malfunctions of the mind due to an underlying disturbance in brain physiology or chemistry. In other words, they are caused by a "broken part" in the brain. These include schizophrenia, bipolar disorder, panic attacks, delirium, autism, clinical depression, or Alzheimer's disease.

- *Dimension:* Some problems aren't best understood as "disease" because they aren't caused strictly by some broken part of the brain. We all have physical traits, like height or weight, or personality traits that vary along a dimension. You can be *more* or *less* sensitive to others' opinions of you, or your intelligence can vary from higher to lower. Some people are challenged because of extreme traits that make it tough to adapt to a world of cultural norms. Examples of this include personality disorders or mental retardation.

- *Behavior:* These are problems we consider *conditioned* and *learned* behaviors, sculpted by experience, by environment, and possibly enhanced by mind-altering substances. There can even be underlying genetics that make a person more vulnerable to being sculpted in certain ways by life experiences. Examples include addiction disorders, eating disorders, and phobias.

- *Life Experiences:* These are problems that can only be understood by looking at the story of a person's life. Sigmund Freud put this way of thinking on the map when he developed psychoanalysis. He believed that dysfunctional life experiences in early life can result in mental health problems later. This view is the basis of many kinds of talk therapies, which have since developed a wide variety of ways to understand the story of a person's life, not just Freud's original way. To help these problems, we have to know the detailed story of a person's life, which, like a good memoir or biography, leads to an understanding of why a problem developed. This is the category that most people think of when they imagine how psychiatrists work, but it is only a way of thinking about certain problems, not all. Hollywood has helped develop this generalization about psychiatry (since a good movie needs a good story). Examples of these kinds of problems include difficulty committing in relationships, problems with authority figures, psychosomatic problems, certain sexual problems, or extreme dependency in a relationship.

In recent years, many neurobiologists, research psychiatrists, psychologists, and addiction specialists have come to learn that most, if not all, psychiatric disorders, including alcohol and drug dependence, are likely the result of a combination of genetic, biological, and environmental factors. With the development of more sophisticated techniques for studying the neurochemistry of the brain, for example, PET (positron emission tomography) and CAT (computerized axial tomography) scans, some disorders that were once seen as strictly caused by family and/or environmental factors, for example, addiction, depression, and even schizophrenia, have been shown to also be associated with alterations in brain chemistry. This finding has been bolstered by the successful treatment of these disorders with medications that put the brain chemistry back into balance with a resulting normalization of the patient's moods and behavior.

Addictions are an interesting area in which our understanding is evolving. They are gradually being included in the category of "diseases." The American Society of Addiction Medicine (www.asam.org) concluded in 2011 that addiction is "not simply a behavior problem involving alcohol, drugs, gambling, or sex. Addiction is a primary, chronic disease of brain reward, motivation, memory, and related circuitry." In fact, conditioned behaviors like addictions can even benefit from certain medications that reduce craving.

It's common for people to have more than one disorder, called *co-occurring disorders, co-morbid disorders,* or sometimes *dual disorders.* For example, because many people with a mental health disorder will self-medicate with alcohol or other drugs, it often happens that they also develop a substance use disorder along with their psychiatric problem. These people will need to be treated for both disorders, ideally at the same time and place, with *integrated treatment.* Unfortunately, such integration is still an ideal toward which the mental health system is striving. It remains fairly common that a person's addiction is treated by addiction specialists in an alcohol and drug treatment program and his or her mental health disorder will be treated separately by a psychiatrist, psychologist, or social worker. In chapter 9, we'll see how the legal system still treats addiction disorders differently from other psychiatric problems.

A Widespread Struggle

A caller to my radio talk show once remarked, "It seems like everyone around me has some kind of mental problem!

Practically everyone I know seems to be depressed, anxious, drinking too much, or using drugs. Is it my imagination or are these problems *that* common?" The fact of the matter is, there *is* a high likelihood that someone you are close to, or work with, has problems of a psychiatric nature. A recent campaign to increase awareness of mental illness by the Maryland Foundation for Psychiatry used the slogan: "Mental Illness Is More Normal Than You Think!"

How likely are these conditions? Ronald Kessler, at the University of Michigan, wanted to know. He interviewed more than nine thousand randomly selected adults, aged fifteen to fifty-four, and found that *nearly half* experienced symptoms at some point that could be diagnosed as a recognized mental disorder severe enough to affect their functioning or well-being. In fact, 30 percent had experienced a diagnosable disorder within the past year.[2] The next time you walk into a roomful of people, look around and think about the fact that *every other person you see* probably has struggled or will eventually struggle with some kind of clinically significant emotional distress or behavioral disorder.

Mental health problems affect all segments of society, regardless of age, gender, education, or ethnicity. In fact, in any six-month period, twenty-five million Americans will have some form of mental disorder; half of these individuals will be children.[3] Surprised? Think about how common it is for things to go wrong in other parts of the human body. For example, about half of Americans suffer from some type of respiratory ailment (emphysema, allergies, etc.), and one out of every five American adults has a cardiovascular condition (heart disease, high blood pressure, etc.).

Mental health problems are not unique to the United States either. The World Health Organization (WHO) has called depression "The Silent Epidemic" and predicts that within twenty years depression will be the largest health burden on societies worldwide.[4]

Under-recognized and Under-treated Problems

Although malfunctioning of the mind/brain is as common as respiratory problems, far fewer people who suffer from mental health problems seek professional, state-of-the-art treatment than do those with emphysema, allergies, or other breathing problems. A study of the Baltimore area showed that nearly one out of three people with a mental disorder were not receiving treatment. This was especially true for alcoholism, which was the most *under-treated* of all problems.[5] Can you imagine what it would be like if one out of three people with diabetes got no medical treatment? The situation would, justifiably, be declared a public health crisis. Of the people in the Baltimore study with clinical depression—a potentially life-threatening condition (in fact, three times more life-threatening than high blood pressure)—fewer than half were getting any kind of treatment.

Particularly ironic is that the people *most* in need of mental health treatment are typically the *least* likely to seek it. For example, a 2009 study in Canada found that only half of those people with thoughts of suicide (or actual plans to commit suicide) sought mental health treatment. When asked why, the most common reason *wasn't* lack of money or access to a psychiatrist; it was, "I preferred to manage the problem myself." This was just as true for those who eventually tried to kill themselves (and survived to be interviewed), as for those merely thinking about it. When looking at people who had received treatment, the study found that many had *delayed* it for years.[6] Another study showed that people who were diagnosed with a mood disorder had put off seeking treatment for six to eight years, and those with anxiety disorders had delayed as long as twenty-three years![7] Certain cultures are less likely to present for treatment than others. For example, Latinos are about half as likely to get treatment for depression or anxiety as the rest of the general population. Interestingly, by comparison, they are *not* less likely to get treatment for substance abuse.

Depression, in particular, is under-recognized and under-treated. Yet depression isn't a rare problem by any means. The National Institute of Mental Health reports that one out of six people will have a serious episode of depression at some point in their lives, and most will have multiple episodes.[8] That's more common than high blood pressure. Mental Health America, a public health research organization, notes, "Despite significant gains in the availability of effective depression treatment over the past decade, the level of unmet need for treatment remains high. On average, people living with depression go for nearly a decade before receiving treatment, and less than one third of people who seek help receive minimally adequate care" (www.mentalhealthamerica.net/go/state-ranking).

The under-recognition and under-treatment of mental disorders is especially a problem among the elderly, where experts estimate that depression is not being treated in up to 90 percent of cases. This is worrisome, as the rate of suicide is rising in the geriatric population four times faster than in the rest of the general population.[9] In Florida, where people over the age of sixty-five make up about 20 percent of the population, a murder-suicide occurs (on average) three times monthly![10] Typically, the murder-suicide is an elderly person killing his spouse before taking his own life. It's not just dementia that is more likely as we get older, but depression, too.

When it comes to getting treatment for emotional and mental health problems, children fare no better than adults. In 2009, the *Omaha World-Herald* reported on the shocking number of "child dumping" cases in Nebraska resulting from the state's "safe haven" drop-off law (which allows parents unable to care for their children to drop them off at a hospital, no questions asked). The report revealed that many of the children abandoned in ERs by their families had serious mental disorders that had never been addressed. These children were hearing voices, acting violently, smearing their own feces on themselves, torturing pets, and making murder and suicide threats. Often, they "didn't appear to get the diagnoses, medication, or other help they needed until after [being dropped off at the] safe haven."[11] Their parents, even those who also struggled with mental health issues, hadn't considered getting professional help for their children, or didn't know how to, or couldn't get as much help as the children needed. Judith Warner wrote in *The New York Times* that many parents share a "popular view that children being labeled mentally ill today are just spirited 'Tom Sawyers' who don't fit our society's cookie-cutter norms, with parents who are desperate to drug them into conformity."[12] The sad experience in Nebraska provides a chilling glimpse into the problem of under-treating psychiatric disorders in children—a subject of entire books (see the resources section on pages 248–253).

As I hope is now clear, the fact that someone you care about is having an emotional or behavioral problem isn't unusual. Nor is the fact that he or she isn't getting any kind of evaluation or treatment for it. But, you should know, there are serious consequences when treatment is delayed.

Untreated Mental Illness: A Danger to Self and Others

Just as there is a wide range of mental health problems, the consequences, when those problems go untreated, vary as well. Often, the troubled person is posing a danger to himself or others. Though some "dangers" can be dramatic—those are the ones that often make the news—more often they are not newsworthy. Nevertheless, they can severely damage the quality of a person's life. In addition, the person with the problem is not the only one affected—other lives are affected, too. The waves of suffering and psychological disturbance radiate outward. Getting *one* person expert help early on can spare the mental health of *many* others. Not all the dangers are strictly physical ones.

Dangers to Self and Others—Non-physical Harm

Since most mental health problems do not result in dramatic or violent changes in behavior, the effects on the sufferers and those around them can be subtle: the failure to receive a promotion at work, erosion of intimate relationships, anxiety and insomnia over the troubled person, the inability to travel far from home, alienation of friends, increasing social isolation, excessive spending on medical visits for elusive physical symptoms, underachievement in activities, highly chaotic living spaces, or financial instability. In these ways, problems in one's mental life can seriously erode quality of life without making headlines.

On the other hand, serious psychiatric disorders can lead to more dire situations: getting fired, getting into accidents, leaving one's family, reckless spending to the point of financial ruin, causing one's children to run away from home, increased risk of teenage pregnancy, aggressive behaviors like "date rape," unnecessary surgeries, eviction from one's apartment, dropping out of school, and a whole host of other instances of being a "danger to self or others" that, while they may not mobilize the authorities or make headlines, are still tragic. These results are loosely measured in the so-called indirect costs of untreated mental illness, often cited as costing Americans nearly $193 billion each year in lost employment, reduced productivity, and public programs that (sometimes) catch the victims of mental illness (and their families) in social welfare safety nets long after problems have escalated.[13] We do know, without doubt, that people with untreated psychiatric problems are at higher risk for these kinds of sad outcomes.

The potential emotional harm that can result from mental illness extends to the family as well. The psychiatric disorder or substance abuse or addiction of *one* person can seriously injure the health of an entire family. For instance, children raised by a depressed parent are often deeply affected psychologically. Neglect, abuse, shaming, and emotional torment are all common experiences for children who have been raised by parents with *untreated* psychiatric problems. A study of the relatives of children admitted to the psychiatric hospital at Cornell White Plains showed that "the parents of children who attempt suicide have significantly higher rates of antisocial personality, assaultive behavior, and substance abuse, compared with the parents of children who did not attempt suicide."[14]

A parent's alcoholism or drug abuse can so psychologically and spiritually wound a child that an enormous national self-help movement has evolved over the last twenty years: Adult Children of Alcoholics (ACOA). Here, in

Twelve Step–type meetings, people share remarkably similar problems within their adult relationships as a result of the wounds sustained growing up in an alcoholic family. Though this phenomenon is not officially recognized in the psychiatrists' diagnostic manual, enough authors have repeatedly cited psychological problems in persons raised by alcoholic parents that most practicing psychotherapists find it helpful to talk of an "ACOA Syndrome." (The direct and indirect dangers of substance abuse are the topics of complete books; between medical mortality and accidents, alcohol abuse accounts for nearly twenty-five thousand deaths a year in the United States.[15])

Study after study has proven that growing up in a home where a parent has untreated mental illness has devastating consequences for a child. In 2010, an in-depth series of articles in the *Los Angeles Times* documented that "growing up with a depressed parent increases a child's risk for mental health problems, cognitive difficulties, and troubled social relationships."[16] Many of the patients I see in my practice as adults are still suffering the effects of having had a parent with untreated mental illness.

Sigmund Freud said that the mind shows itself in two great domains of functioning—love and work. Clearly, the ravages of mental disorders show up in both of those places. Jordan's is a typical case.

• JORDAN •

Jordan's parents were concerned. His high school grades were dropping, and he was becoming more withdrawn and irritable. Up until the last few months, he had been a quiet, friendly boy—"no trouble." Something in him had changed. He had become so short-tempered that his girlfriend had broken up with him; she couldn't take his explosiveness any more. His parents suspected he was using drugs and even had his urine tested, but it was clean. They didn't know what to do, but they told Jordan they were always open to talk about things. Jordan didn't know how to talk about how he was feeling, but he knew how to express his feelings in other ways—he began cutting himself. Tensions over Jordan were straining his parents' relationship. They fought over what to do and, a few times, his father threatened to leave.

A decline in schoolwork, loss of a girlfriend, social withdrawal, a noticeable alteration in mood—these are typical signs for an adolescent who may be developing a mood disorder, which, in most cases starts between ages seventeen and twenty-four. Jordan's parents were conflicted about how best to help their son, and their arguments were taking a toll on their marriage. At this point, Jordan needed professional evaluation and treatment.

Consider how often people are concerned enough to have their blood pressure checked. Yet, the chances of dying from elevated blood pressure within the first few years of its detection are about fifty times lower than the risk of dying from untreated depression! When depression is treated, the likelihood of suicide is decreased dramatically—by a factor of ten. The risks of no treatment are many and serious, including death.

Danger to Self and Others—Physical Harm

What does it mean when a person with mental illness presents a physical danger to others? Usually, this starts with frightening threats and then escalates to assault, or worse.

Anyone paying attention to the news is aware of the dreadfully violent "danger to others" outcomes of untreated mental illness. Thankfully, this kind of violence *is* rare, occurring in fewer than one in one hundred mental illness cases. The majority of mentally ill people who commit extremely violent acts have either never been in treatment or had dropped out of it. Only 10 percent of all homicides are committed by people with serious mental illness, and of those most were *not* in treatment. Although usually associated with *severe* mental illness like schizophrenia or manic depression, violence is actually more common with mental health problems like substance abuse and personality disorders, especially when both are combined.[17]

Psychiatrist and activist E. Fuller Torrey points out that, sometimes, violence that appears to be political is really motivated by delusions and related mental symptoms.[18] For example, in 1980, former congressman Allard Lowenstein was assassinated by Dennis Sweeny, who believed the congressman had implanted a radio transmitter in his teeth. In 1988, Russell Weston, acting on his schizophrenic delusion that the government had a secret time-machine in the U. S. Capitol, shot two guards in the Capitol building. Jared Lee Loughner, who shot Congresswoman Gabrielle Giffords in 2011, was motivated by paranoid ideas about government—"mind control and brainwashing efforts," as he called it in a YouTube rant. Sadly, his college had sent him home because of his psychiatric symptoms, but he never got treatment.

The news stories that garner the most attention are about violence that occurs in public locations, like the massacre at Virginia Tech in 2007. But the violence is usually closer to home. In a 1990 survey, the National Alliance on

Mental Illness (NAMI) randomly selected 1,401 families of people with severe mental illness; 12 percent reported that their ill family members had threatened to harm another person, and 11 percent had actually harmed someone at some point during their illness. Again, physical violence is not common with mental health problems, but when it does occur it is most often (65 percent of the time) directed toward a family member.[19]

It's also important to recognize that not just the victim and his or her family suffer when a mentally ill person acts violently; an entire community's mental health can be affected. Two months after the Virginia Tech shooting, 15 percent of the student body were struggling with a psychiatric disorder known as post-traumatic stress disorder (PTSD), 5 percent of which was considered "very serious." Only one in ten of these students got professional help; yet three times as many reported that they could have used help but couldn't or wouldn't reach out to obtain it.[20]

The danger to one's self that mental illness can cause is sadly familiar to many. This danger can take the form of suicidal threats or acts. For people diagnosed with clinical depression alone, 15 percent will attempt suicide if their depression goes untreated. Of these, about fifteen in one hundred will be successful in killing themselves. That is a staggering statistic. It translates into the incredible fact that suicide is the *eighth* leading cause of death in America, and second only to car accidents in teenagers between ages fifteen and nineteen. In fact, on average, thirty college-aged people die by their own hands in this country every day. Even so, the age group with the highest suicide rate is the elderly, of whom over six thousand die by suicide each year.[21] This is especially tragic if we consider that the majority—

over 80 percent—of these suicides could have been prevented with just a few weeks of treatment! How many of these deaths could have been prevented if someone who cared had seen the warning signs and had tried to lead the suffering person into state-of-the-art treatment?

There are less obvious physical dangers—behaviors that may not attract legal attention and call out judges, magistrates, police, and emergency room physicians. Harming one's self can also be a result of neglect. People with psychiatric disorders often ignore their physical health. If they have a medical problem, like diabetes for example, it may be dangerously neglected. A study within the VA (Department of Veterans Affairs) health care system of over 175,000 patients showed that "patients with diabetes or hypertension who had been diagnosed with schizophrenia, bipolar disorder, or an anxiety disorder had substantially fewer visits [for their diabetes or hypertension] than those who did not have these psychiatric diagnoses." Patients older than fifty with a diagnosis of substance abuse, depression, bipolar or anxiety disorder, or post-traumatic stress disorder were less likely to have *any* medical care at all.[22]

Indeed, the dangers of untreated mental disorders are many. The good news is that most of these dangers are potentially preventable with treatment. If so, why aren't troubled or suffering people seeking professional evaluation and treatment? The next chapter reviews some of the numerous reasons—many of which probably apply to the troubled person you are trying to help.

3

Why Mental Illness Goes Untreated

"The less we know, the longer our explanations."
— EZRA POUND

As the previous chapter illustrates, mental illnesses are common. You now know that the situation you're facing is *not* unique, and that the fallout of allowing the problem to continue unaddressed can be serious. Why, then, does mental illness go untreated? Why don't those who suffer with a problem in thoughts, feelings, or behaviors seek treatment?

When it comes to any health matter, we know people (including ourselves) who delay medical attention for physical problems—a bad knee, a growth, even chest pain. Yet resistance to seeking professional help for mental problems is even higher.

It's a delicate word, "mental." It's used as an insult among kids on the playground and, even in adult life, we sprinkle it into our conversations as a pejorative. Who knows how that misuse evolved? Nonetheless, it remains a loaded word, and one that can elicit a defensive response. No wonder you have been reluctant to start a conversation about your friend's mental state. Yet the adjective itself, "mental" (as in mental health), comes from the Latin *mentalis*, which means "of the mind." We *should* consider it a benign word that simply identifies an important part of the human experience.

That said, many issues prevent a person from realizing or admitting that psychiatric treatment is needed. Stigma, denial, gender, the disease itself—all commonly play a role. Typically, a combination of factors (sociological, psychological, biological, and financial) collectively keeps a person from seeking help for a mental health problem. Of these, the most common is social or cultural.

Social and Cultural Factors

The United States was founded by refugees and immigrants. Very often, these were exceptionally brave people who took action to escape social oppression, religious persecution, and other forms of domination. Puritanism, in particular, was the religion the earliest settlers brought to the colonies of the New World. The Puritans established the first formal governments here, and the moral structure of the emerging society. Self-reliance and the sublimation of feelings into productive work were strong Puritan values. These were also helpful for survival in the harsh and hostile settlements of New England: the soil was difficult to cultivate, the natives presented a threat, and the winters took many lives. What a person made, built, or grew were of vital importance. When humans are in "survival mode," what we *accomplish* is far more important than what we *feel*. Every soldier on the battlefield who has lost a friend under fire knows, in that situation, even grief is a luxury. In the cradle of our history, there was far more room for *doing* than for *feeling*.

The Puritan virtues that encourage industriousness, entrepreneurialism, and initiative (and which have led to many accomplishments in this country) have vulnerabilities as well. In particular, a focus on outward achievements takes attention away from inner life—the life of feelings, emotions, personal thoughts, and self-reflection.

Other cultural forces play a role in this outward focus. For example, it has always been harder for men to focus inward than for women, as social pressures have encouraged tangible achievements from men. Today, the highly stimulating media of television and the Internet cultivate a short attention span and decimate time for reflection. In fact, the majority of our national pastimes have moved from inward-looking activities such as reading, writing, and contemplation to focusing on other people's stories, troubles, and "news." As the amount of leisure time for Americans has grown, so has our average hours-per-week of television watching and time online. The renowned Dr. Benjamin Spock observed, "It seems hard for children just to be by themselves, to sit under a tree, and enjoy the world. There's a constant need to keep doing, to keep going, to keep life stimulating at all times—and usually that involves electronics or the TV screen."

Noises in the outer world can easily drown out the more subtle sound of our inner lives. And as we become deaf to this inner music, we may also develop the illusion that there is simply very little to our inner lives. As a result, we're much more likely to focus on the outside world instead of looking inward at our feelings. We may fail to notice that something might be "out of sync" in our brains, creating disorder and chaos in our minds, bleeding into our everyday lives.

Seeking psychiatric help is an acknowledgement that there is something "inner," an interior dimension known mostly to the self and largely unseen by others. In that sense it is so ineffable or intangible that it seems less "real," especially in a social environment that is focused on *doing* rather than *being*. Critics have accused our culture of being "self-absorbed." While that may be true, it's not the same as being *self-aware*. It is uncomfortable in our culture to focus inward, and that becomes even more off-putting if what we see is not flattering or brings emotional pain. In our outward-focused culture, aberrant *behaviors* are easier to observe and acknowledge than inner pain. Perhaps that is why, in recent years, it has become more customary to refer to psychiatric treatment as *"behavioral* health treatment," emphasizing the more observable and comfortable domain of *behavior* over thoughts or feelings.

Free Will and the Illusion of Control

In addition to our society's admiration for self-reliance, and on *doing* rather than feeling, many assume that our "conscious will" is always in control of our thoughts, feelings, and behaviors. In America, in particular, we are determined to celebrate our will, its power, its determination, and its ability to direct and control all decisions in our lives. Being in control of one's faculties, using our minds to make our bodies do the things we want is greatly admired in our culture. We want to be able to solve those difficult math problems in school, or take that jump shot at the hoop with accuracy and grace, or play the piano well. In contrast, the failure to exercise one's will causes shame, whether it's sticking to a diet, avoiding impulsive decisions, or failing to keep our commitments. We live in Nike times:

"Just Do It!" We tied an entire campaign to curtail drug use in young people to the very American slogan, "Just Say No!" The operative word here is *just*. It implies that will-power is almighty, and that making a decision to change is a simple matter.

Scientific evidence suggests that believing our actions are "willed" might even be an illusion. In his book *The Mind's Past*, Michael S. Gazzaniga presents neuroscientific evidence that a large number of the decisions we ascribe to conscious free will are actually executed in other parts of the brain, long before a person claims to have consciously "decided" to take an action. In other words, what appears to be a conscious decision is sometimes literally an "after-thought" of processes that started beneath the level of conscious awareness. Yet our *psychological* need to feel that our will is all-powerful persists.

What does this have to do with the reluctance to seek mental health care? Whether we are hardwired to believe we are in control, or whether we have developed this stance via our culture, we despise anything that threatens our sense of being in control of our *mental* processes. It is no wonder that anything that threatens the notion of free will is frightening to us. The age-old fear of "madness" is based on the loss of control of one's mental faculties, particularly the will.

In twenty-five years of practicing psychiatry, some of the most effective approaches for change that I have come across are the Twelve Step programs for addictive behaviors used by Alcoholics Anonymous (AA), Narcotics Anonymous (NA), Sexaholics Anonymous (SA), and many others, includ-ing the programs for people in relationships with addicts, such as Al-Anon, Narc-Anon, S-Anon, and Co-Dependents

Anonymous (CoDA). All of these self-help support groups run on the basic formula of the Twelve Steps. The Steps are not only a recipe for maintaining abstinence from an addiction but also a fairly sound formula for personal growth. This formula incorporates the basic wisdoms of many theories of human psychology. Of the Twelve Steps, the First is possibly the most profound:

> **Step One:** We admitted we were powerless over [insert drug or behavior of choice here]—that our lives had become unmanageable.

On the surface, Step One appears like a paradox. How can admitting powerlessness be a step toward change, to taming an uncontrolled behavior? This is the approach of taking one step back (powerlessness) to go two steps forward (empowerment). This is a deeply significant idea and I see it as the key to why Twelve Step programs are so successful. Implicit in this statement is the idea that something is happening that the will cannot fully control. The profound admission in the First Step is that the will has *tried* to control a problem and has *failed*. This is indeed a powerful realization: the will is limited, it has been tested to its limits, and, though perhaps necessary, it's *not sufficient* to conquer the problem unaided.

The Second of the Twelve Steps goes on from there:

> **Step Two:** We came to believe that a Power greater than ourselves could restore us to sanity.

The will is simply not all-powerful, not enough to bring us back to health without *some kind of additional help*. The help can come in many forms, and there are many powers "greater than ourselves": professional therapy, medications, fellowship—all "higher" powers than unaided will. The Twelve Step programs tackle the problem right at its root: the limitation of *will*. In these meetings, many ideas are discussed that reflect Step Two. Concepts such as arrogance, humility, and surrender are deeply familiar talking points to anyone who has attended Twelve Step meetings.

Fear of confronting the limitations of the will is a major factor in why people avoid treatment for a mental health problem. In particular, the idea of taking psychiatric medication is, for many, the ultimate admission that one's will is limited. The effectiveness of medication does indeed suggest that a (neurochemical) power outside of will alone is at work. Unfortunately, many people fear that imposing an external agent to help change mental life replaces free will with a "chemical patch." This reaction is common; helping patients deal with it is a critical part of prescribing psychiatric medication. Medication is not a "crutch." It can be an important, even essential, part of treatment and healing.

Some Mental Illnesses Can Impair Insight

Sometimes the obstacle to seeking treatment is the mental disorder itself. Some disorders impair a person's ability to look at himself or herself objectively. In psychiatry, we call this: "lack of insight." It is a common symptom. The technical term for this is *anosognosia*.

Explaining how the phenomenon of "mind" arises from the functioning of brain cells is one of the staggering challenges modern neuroscientists face. But there is fairly universal agreement that the brain is the organ that generates all mental functioning. Most of the brain's functions are entirely automatic and involve making continuous adjustments in various parts of the body, completely outside our awareness and not requiring our attention. One of the brain's monitoring functions, which seems to be unique to human consciousness, is the ability to self-observe—to identify that there is a *self*, to know what that self is thinking and feeling, and to make specific decisions about how to behave. Many psychologists have studied the mind's self-observing ability, such as when it develops in children or how it relates to other mental functions. Some scientists think they may have detected the ability to self-observe in chimpanzees and elephants, thus raising the question whether this ability *is* unique to humans.

Modern brain-imaging techniques demonstrate that certain regions of the brain are connected with specific mental processes. In this way, researchers have been able to determine which brain circuits are involved with insight and self-observation. The anterior medial frontal cortex, located near the front of the brain, seems especially important. It turns out that some psychiatric disorders, particularly those that involve biological malfunctioning of the brain such as mania and schizophrenia, can cause the circuits that self-observe to go haywire. Much research has been done to explore this strange and vexing aspect of these diseases, because this particular symptom is especially predictive of poor outcomes and problematic behaviors, including violence.

Lack of insight, *anosognosia*, is uniquely tragic—everyone can see the problem *except* the ill person. It's why people with this condition so often think that *others* are crazy for calling them ill. This is one of the most stressful symptoms for family members.[23] This is also a challenge for the clinicians who treat people with certain disorders, especially schizophrenia. It's not that they *won't* admit they need help; it's that they *can't* admit it. They will not come for treatment, at times have to be forced into treatment (see chapters 8 and 9), and may not stick with important medication. *They don't think anything is wrong with them.* Some may be engaged in outrageous behaviors: running around the streets naked, masturbating in public, collecting their feces in plastic bags, tearing up the house looking for phone taps and electronic bugs, or talking loudly to invisible voices. Yet, they don't consider these behaviors abnormal in any way. Landlords are incensed, families are mortified, neighbors are frightened, but the person herself doesn't see any problem with her behavior. In fact, the person may believe that the problem lies with others. We may say that they are "suffering" from an illness, but the sick person may not be experiencing any suffering at all. In fact, someone who is manic may be having the time of his life—while unwittingly causing others to suffer deeply.

Hallucinations, delusions, and lack of insight into being sick are classic examples of mental symptoms that you, the well person, can observe, but the sick person cannot. You can self-observe. You know what is normal, what your usual state of health is, and when you need help. A person with schizophrenia, however, who hears voices coming from the heating vent, or whispering in her ear, sees no such thing. She doesn't see that there is something strange, unreal, or sick about this. For her, the voice is totally real. Remember, the brain is what is ill—the very organ we use to self-observe.

It is fascinating that a person with schizophrenia can function rationally in other areas—can still drive a car, trace an electrical problem to a blown fuse, stop at a red light, balance a checkbook, and so on. But, when it comes to dealing

with symptoms of the disease, the person's rational thinking breaks down. Instead of explaining a hallucination as
a sign of mental malfunctioning, the schizophrenic's mind
applies far more twisted explanations. Hence, *delusional*
thinking often accompanies hallucinations. Though common
in schizophrenia, hallucinations and delusions can also be
seen in other types of mental illness.

Denial

"There is nothing wrong with me," a man said to me during
our first meeting. His wife insisted he see me because he
was crying constantly during the day, and occasionally missing work because of his crying. It didn't take a psychiatrist
to see the man was in denial. Denial is a far less serious
phenomenon than psychosis, and more mild than anosognosia, because it can be more easily addressed. Denial, by the
way, is not unique to mental health problems; people ignore
chest pains, bad coughs, lumps in the breast, or other physical symptoms all the time.

What does it mean to be in *denial?* In psychology, denial
refers to an automatic mental process (quite natural in the
human mind) that deals with fear by ignoring a problem.
Denial can be helpful in some cases, especially in a time of
crisis, when we need to address a problem promptly and the
fear may be paralyzing. There is a time and place for healthy
denial. But in matters of health, including mental health,
denial is out of place and even harmful. Whereas lack of
insight is common with schizophrenia, denial is common in
less severe psychiatric problems such as depression and
addictions. Interestingly, it is the least problem in anxiety
disorders—those patients suffer, know they suffer, and want
help. Unfortunately, their anxiety makes them scared of

taking the medications or engaging in the behavioral therapies that can be the most effective and bring them the quickest relief.

Sometimes we don't deny things as much as we minimize them: "It's not so bad." "It will get better on its own." "It could be worse." "I can handle it." Yet this approach can be more dangerous. Acknowledging that there may be a problem but behaving as though "everything is under control" can backfire. If the problem gets worse, the implication is that you failed to control it. One of the reasons we use denial is to cover our fear of failure, incompetence, or ignorance. Strong cultural forces shame us for such things, often starting early in life.

Both outright denial and minimization prevent people from seeing things as they are, acknowledging a problem, exposing vulnerability, and getting help. But to feel *less* vulnerable, you may have to feel *more* vulnerable first. One of the great psychologists of the early twentieth century, Carl Jung, was interested in paradoxes like this and how they can be used to help people psychologically. He wrote: "It is a bewildering thing in human life that the thing that causes the great fear is the source of great wisdom. One's greatest foolishness is one's biggest stepping stone. Nobody can become a wise man without first being a terrible fool."[24] Jung knew that admitting we have a problem, that we may be weak, and that we don't know enough to solve it on our own is the most effective first step in moving forward.

Stigma

We live in a society that is much more comfortable dealing with physical problems than emotional problems. With physical problems, we can talk about *illness, sickness,* or *disease.* When it comes to problems in our mental lives, however, other words creep in, even if we don't say them aloud: *weakness, stupidity, cowardice,* and even *weird, crazy,* or *insane.* If we are being politically correct, we'll say "troubled" or "challenged" or that a person "has issues." However you look at it, the fact remains that a stigma is attached to acknowledging or having mental health problems.

Webster's Dictionary defines stigma as a Greek word meaning "a mark, sign, etc., of disgrace . . . or that something is not considered normal or standard." Since Biblical times, abnormal behaviors have often carried a stigma. In her superb book, *Helping Someone with Mental Illness,* Rosalynn Carter gives a short history of stigma:

> [In ancient Greek times] "madness," although viewed as caused by capricious gods, was a source of shame . . . Even in more modern times, mental illnesses were thought to be caused by possession by the devil. According to Norman Dain, professor of history at Rutgers University, "The traditional belief among Christians that madness is often a punishment visited by God on the sinner predominated in American society during the 17th century and remained quite influential thereafter." . . . Pennsylvania Hospital was one of the first general hospitals in colonial America to admit "lunatics" . . . the public was allowed to come on weekends to view the "lunatics"—for a small fee! With this kind of a past, we can easily understand why there is stigma associated with mental illness.[25]

The stigma associated with mental illness can be blamed for the general reluctance to seek psychiatric evaluation. Who wants to have a condition that, for centuries, has meant being an outcast? The good news is that many organizations are working to combat stigma: the American Psychiatric Association, Mental Health America, the National Alliance on Mental Illness; and even Rotary, a community service organization, has a national "Erase the Stigma Campaign." Particular credit should be given to the Mental Health Program at the Carter Center in Atlanta, under the leadership of Rosalynn Carter. It has even established a fellowship for journalists to learn about psychiatric disorders to foster the accurate portrayal of the mentally ill in the media, and it has taken on a leadership role in public education.

Real improvements in the efficacy of psychiatric treatment are changing attitudes toward treatment for mental health problems. We have more rapid ways of helping people feel better, or to change behavior, than years of analysis on the couch. Perhaps it's because we are starting to identify certain disorders (like depression, schizophrenia, panic disorder, even addictions) as brain *diseases*, so there is less tendency to see them as weaknesses. Whatever the reason, although still a problem, the stigma isn't what it used to be and this means more people are willing to seek help.

Helping to erode stigma are some broad public efforts to heighten awareness of the signs of emotional disturbance and its treatability (and prevent its horrible consequences, such as suicide), particularly within groups that have been traditionally resistant to getting treatment, such as law enforcement. The National Police Suicide Foundation, formed in response to an increasing rate of suicide among the police force in recent years, especially in certain states, is a terrific example. The newest frontier in battling stigma is in the military, where suicide rates have been soaring since the Iraq war; some months, suicides have outnumbered combat casualties. Vigorous anti-stigma campaigns in the Army are associating the courage to get mental health treatment with inner strength.

Misinformation about Psychiatrists

Today, much of our general knowledge comes from the media, particularly from television and movies. If you have never been to a psychiatrist and your impression is based on what you have seen in the movies, you probably have a frightening and inaccurate picture, one that would be a further hurdle to seeking professional medical help for a mental problem.

In my opinion, the distortions created by Hollywood about mental illness, its treatment, and its care providers are so great they must be a factor in people's decisions to avoid treatment. This effect of media is so significant it is discussed by psychiatrists in professional journals. George Gerbner, professor of communications and emeritus dean of the Annenberg School for Communications, found that television, even more than films, presented inaccurate portrayals of mental illness.[26] For example, one study showed that 77 percent of the mentally ill depicted on TV were violent, whereas in real life violence occurs typically in under 10 percent of the mentally ill.[27]

Old Ideas versus New Ideas

In his book *Freudian Fraud: The Malignant Effect of Freudian Theory on American Culture,* E. Fuller Torrey asserts that Freudian psychoanalytic theory took a negative toll on our society's view of mental health care. In particular, he believes it tried to explain too much: criminal acts, war, and all manner of disturbing behavior. In short, says Torrey, psychoanalytic psychiatry oversold itself. Freudian theory also led the average person to conclude that any kind of abnormal feeling, thought, or behavior was loaded with implications from the past and fraught with unconscious meanings. The idea that examination of any psychiatric problem could become a door that opens up deep, dark, long-repressed secrets is intimidating to many people. Some people incorrectly believe that this kind of laborious, prob-ing psychoanalysis is still the dominant method used, which leads them to avoid seeking treatment, feeling that it will inevitably "open a can of worms."

Psychotherapy received bad press again in the late 1990s, reinforcing the idea that therapy can uncover frightening secrets we may not even be aware of. This was the scandalous phenomenon of "recovered memories." Some therapists claim to have revealed severe traumas of horrible abuse in childhood, memories that were completely forgotten or "repressed" by the patient before treatment. A controversy rages over this issue, with a minority of therapists insisting that such memories "uncovered" during treatment are "real." Most therapists, particularly hard-core cognitive and memory neuropsychologists, say that, based on research of how human memory is encoded and retrieved, this is very unlikely. This controversy has been the topic of entire books, and a detailed discussion is outside the scope of this book. Unfortunately, it fuels the fires of fear and keeps some people from seeking treatment.

Civil Rights

• CLARISSA •

Clarissa was thirty-four, and a regular in the downtown Baltimore shelter. She pushed around a shopping cart overflowing with old stuffed animals that she picked up at various shelters, where they had been donated for children. She usually wore many layers of clothing, a wardrobe for each season of the year, even in the hottest weather. The stuffed animals and her clothes were stained and shredded from months of exposure to the weather. She spent much of her day talking to her stuffed animals, and hearing them talk back, convinced that they were protecting her from the attempts of her family and the government to implant a poison pellet in her brain. As long as she kept close to her animals, and away from anything institutional— hospitals, group homes, relief agencies of any sort—she thought she would be safe. The shelter was the only facility she could tolerate. She was receiving no psychiatric treatment, and taking no medication.

Gradually, her paranoid ideas grew so severe that she wouldn't go into a shelter. Many attempts had been made to coax her into treatment at a health clinic for the homeless in Baltimore, but she refused. Her refusal had to be honored since, legally, in Maryland (as in most states), unless she were imminently dangerous to herself or others, she had the right to refuse treatment. She slept on the streets. One night, following a freak cold front that had blown in, Clarissa was found in her shopping cart, frozen to death. When I worked in a clinic serving homeless persons I learned a term that workers there have for this kind of outcome, "Dying with your rights on."

Ironically, civil rights legislation, one of the greatest social achievements of twentieth-century America, has had the unintended consequence of allowing mentally ill people to refuse needed treatment. Civil rights, when mixed with denial or lack of insight, has created a cocktail of avoidance that accounts for too many missed opportunities for psychiatric treatment. Because of the narrow criteria that allow over-riding an individual's civil right to refuse treatment, family, community leaders, and even the police are sometimes left to stand by and watch while people with mental illnesses deteriorate, until they cross a legally defined threshold of dangerous—at which point it may be too late. It's not uncommon, despite the best efforts of families and health care workers, to face tremendous challenges in getting extremely troubled people into a psychiatric hospital against their will. When involuntary commitment hearings are pursued, public defenders will argue to defend a patient's right to refuse treatment, even if it's at the expense of that person's health. For better or worse, that is the American system. (This scenario is explored in more detail in chapter 9, where we will look at ways to overcome these obstacles.)

The Special Challenge for Men Seeking Help

Men are particularly reluctant to show up for psychiatric treatment. This is true for men in general, and for male-dominated professions (like law enforcement and the military) in particular. Most psychiatrists see two to three times as many women as men in their practice. Why? There are lots of explanations, but most boil down to cultural factors. Boys in our contemporary society commonly learn that being a man requires toughness, self-reliance, and dealing with painful emotions by ignoring them. Deborah Tannen, in her groundbreaking studies of the different ways men and women communicate and deal with emotional issues, has pointed out that men are more oriented to fixing, repairing, and solving problems while women are more apt to share feelings for the purposes of making a connection. Men like to *give* help, but not *get* it. How easy is it for many men to ask for directions when lost? Settings that require disclosure of feelings, especially to another man, are not comfortable for men. For many, it is particularly uncomfortable to appear vulnerable, imperfect, frightened, or not in control.

Across cultures, a central feature of manhood is the role of protecting *others* from their fears—women and children in particular. Who, then, protects a man from his fears? For most men, it's a do-it-yourself job. Men often learn from watching each other that they must deal with their fears alone. You can see why, then, the mind of a man is primed for denial of vulnerability and for minimizing emotional trouble; he must be able to focus on the fears of others. In my clinical experience, these generalizations (and they are generalizations) are just as true of gay men as of straight men.

There is a greater than even chance that the person you are trying to help is a man. Men are notorious for avoiding medical attention, especially for preventive care. Maybe that's why they do not live as long as women—seven years less, on average. In a survey conducted by *Men's Health* magazine and CNN, nearly thirty-two million men at any given time are avoiding visits to a doctor's office for health maintenance. Nearly 25 percent of men surveyed had not been in for a regular age-appropriate checkup (e.g., prostate exam, blood pressure check, colon cancer screening, diabetes evaluation) in two years or more, and 20 percent in five years or more. Some cited lack of time, others said "only sick people go to the doctor." One out of every four men said they did not trust doctors, and half of them said that any problem that might be uncovered would be incurable anyway.[28] This is similar to the findings of studies about why people don't seek professional help for "psychological distress"; they think treatment doesn't work, problems will go away by themselves eventually, they can handle their problems without outside help, or "anyone" should be able to cope with these difficulties. Many of these "reasons" are transparent excuses; some even border on the irrational, and thus constitute *denial*—sticking your head in the sand and pretending nothing is wrong.

Personality Factors

We all know people who find it hard to admit they are having a problem or admit mistakes. For some, being independent, self-sufficient, a "do-it-yourselfer" is practically a religion. This isn't really a mental illness in its own right; it's an enduring set of traits. Sometimes these traits can be assets, such as being able to work productively alone. At other times, however, these traits are a liability. They can make a person reluctant to seek treatment, and they can complicate the treatment itself—if and when that person shows up for it.

In fact, what makes us unique as individuals is our own personal collection of enduring traits, a profile of characteristics by which we are known to our friends, families, and coworkers. Personality traits that might make a person

averse to seeking professional mental health help, even
when suffering, commonly include

- perfectionism
- a high level of expressed anger
- a need for control
- a tendency to be uncomfortable with dependence
  on others

These same personality traits also happen to be linked
with ignoring and minimizing chest pain, which is likely to
indicate a heart problem. However, in certain contexts, they
can be assets and important strengths—careers have been
built on them. But at other times they can be problems, and
not just in the context of needing psychiatric help. (A paradox I have often observed is that the same set of traits, so
helpful in the workplace, can sometimes cause real problems at home, in family relationships.)

The good news is that if people with some of these
personality traits can be drafted into psychiatric treatment,
a variety of treatment techniques are available to accommodate them. There are now over three hundred recognized
treatment techniques, so there are plenty to choose from.
People with certain personality characteristics do better
with some techniques than with others. Perfectionists, once
in psychiatric treatment, are sometimes the hardest-working
patients in therapy, always trying to be "A+ students" in the
face of a demanding new activity. They take the project
of treatment seriously, often educating themselves about
their conditions (which is always empowering), and they can
challenge the care provider in productive and creative ways.

For certain disorders, treatments are effective regardless of the personality features of the patients. Other
studies have found that personality traits that predict

success in treatment for men are different than those for women. Today's mental health providers receive training in many different techniques and will work to match techniques to personality traits.

The Culture of the "Maalox Moment"

When I present a lecture to physicians or the general public, I often remind the audience that we live in a culture of expectations primed by TV advertising. Think of ads that feature a ticking clock showing how it takes only a few seconds for an antacid or headache pill to provide relief! We have even come to expect that a course of antibiotics for bronchitis, a urinary tract infection, strep throat, or other common ailments will take only a few days to provide complete relief. Our expectations are high for short-term gains that come quickly and relatively easily—relief in a "Maalox Moment."

Though a few mental problems can respond relatively quickly to certain medications (attention deficit disorder is one example), most psychiatric problems require more time to treat. They often take many months or, sometimes, even years. After all, problems in the area of emotions, behaviors, or thoughts can take many years to develop. It should be no surprise that they may take a while to improve. Some mental health problems are similar to chronic medical problems, like diabetes or arthritis, in that they are enduring and will require lifelong visits to the doctor. Illnesses such as schizophrenia, borderline personality disorder, obsessive compulsive disorder, and most (but not all) cases of depression or manic depression are chronic brain diseases with periods of both remission and relapse, and they require ongoing contact with one or more expert providers.

Much of our medical system, as well as our typical mind-set, focuses on short-term conditions. It's tempting to see health problems as either "curable" or "terminal." The majority of health care dollars in the United States, however, are not spent in *either* of those two categories, but in a third: "treatable." These illnesses are not curable, but with ongoing treatment can result in reasonable health, longer life spans, and good functioning (common examples include back pain, arthritis, irritable bowel syndrome, prostate enlargement, diabetes, high blood pressure, coronary artery disease, and a surprisingly large variety of cancers). Most mental health problems fall into this category as well. The medical challenge of the twentieth century was to address acute conditions and find cures for them—mostly infectious disease and trauma. In the twenty-first century, chronic diseases and their "management" have moved to center stage.

Even psychiatric problems that can be treated on a short-term basis and do not require lifetime treatment, such as clinical depression, often take many months to treat. Medications such as antidepressants take a *minimum* of six to eight weeks to have full effect. No "Maalox Moment" here. In fact, it is possible for the depression to get *worse* while waiting for the medicine to kick in. Even after depression remits, the antidepressant needs to be continued for at least a year, or there is significant risk of relapse.

Whether acute (like clinical depression) or chronic (like schizophrenia), psychiatric treatment requires commitment, patience, and more perseverance than most people consider when thinking about medical care. The prospect of sticking with treatment for a while is daunting to many, and discourages some from even starting.

One more point is worth considering in this regard. Not

only do psychiatric treatments take longer than Maalox, they also require more from the person being treated. A common vision of modern medical treatment is that something is done by a doctor *to* you. You take a pill, and simply wait. You go in for surgery and sleep while the problem is surgically fixed. All you have to do is eat, drink, urinate, and walk, like you normally do, in the subsequent days to gradually recover from what was done *to* you. Mental health treatment, in contrast, asks for more participation, engagement, and effort from the patient. Knowing this can be off-putting. Psychiatric treatment has more in common with, say, physical therapy than with surgery or a medical treatment from your family physician.

Manifestations: Physical Symptoms Due to Emotional Problems

Emotional distress can be manifested in many ways. One particularly common way mental distress is expressed is with physical symptoms. There is a very real connection between mind and body.

Every primary care physician knows that a certain percentage of patients who show up at the office with physical problems are actually suffering from psychiatric conditions. This doesn't mean that "it's all in their heads." Mental health conditions can cause real physical symptoms such as headaches, palpitations, constipation, diarrhea, stomach aches, and heartburn—all common complaints of people with clinical depression or anxiety disorders. In one study, up to 26 percent of patients in a typical primary care office practice had a psychiatric disorder, which was often the very cause of the physical problems for which they were seeking care. About half of these patients were clinically depressed.[29]

Just as many physical disorders can have psychiatric symptoms (cancer can cause depression, for example, sometimes even before a person knows he or she has cancer), so, too, can many mental disorders cause physical symptoms. When I was an intern in internal medicine at Johns Hopkins, a number of the patients I saw had no significant physical causes for their physical complaints, but they did have psychiatric conditions that explained them. The way mental and physical symptoms are so interrelated leads many patients away from necessary psychiatric attention. Often people who need mental health treatment instead show up in medical clinics ready to spend time, energy, and money tracking down physical causes of their symptoms, thinking they are "getting help." But sometimes it is not the right kind of help.

Often, unfortunately, primary care practitioners (PCPs) do not pick up on a psychiatric problem when patients come to them with primarily physical symptoms. Many studies show that PCPs fail to recognize psychiatric disorders in their patients as much as 40 percent of the time.[30] Consequently, a great deal of medical time and energy can be spent by non-psychiatrists on such patients before the psychiatric problem is actually addressed. In extreme cases, people even have unnecessary surgeries for vague complaints of back, abdominal, or pelvic pain—pain that is really related to a psychiatric disorder. Others have plastic surgery to treat a particular mental illness known as "body dysmorphic disorder" that is far better treated by therapy and psychiatric medications.

Financial Barriers

Every year, I participate in an event called National Depression Screening Day. It is usually the first Thursday in

October, and free depression screenings are given in malls, clinics, hospitals, and hotels at thousands of sites around the country. The event draws people who are not currently receiving mental health treatment but who wonder if they should be, because they are feeling bad emotionally. It's a chance to meet people who have been contemplating evaluation and treatment, or who might be on the verge of it but haven't taken that step. They will, however, come to a free health screening. They fill out a questionnaire and then have it scored by a psychiatrist who discusses the results with them. Some of the questions try to find out what a person thinks and feels about psychiatric consultations, and, if he or she hasn't gotten one yet, why not? Perhaps the single-most-common reason cited for postponing a consultation is money.

Many people believe they cannot afford mental health treatment or they don't have adequate insurance coverage. In fact, health insurance policies discriminated against mental health treatment for a long time, covering such visits at a lower rate than other kinds of health care treatments.

Historically, whether they could afford it or not, some people *required* psychiatric treatment, particularly the seriously mentally ill. The "public mental health system" was developed, which consisted of inpatient facilities for the seriously ill (which were often called "state mental hospitals") and community-based clinics that gave care on a sliding scale. Meanwhile, the development of HMOs made *some* mental health care available to people who previously did not have access to it. Prior to HMOs, it was possible to have medical insurance that simply had no benefits for psychiatric treatments. Now, HMOs almost universally include some benefit for these kinds of problems. Today, in an

HMO, you can see a mental health provider for the same kind of co-pay (typically $30) that applies to your primary care physician.

For some years, there has been a legislative push in many states, and nationally, to establish "parity" for mental health benefits. Parity means covering emotional and mental problems (including substance abuse) the same way other illnesses are covered—the same co-pays, the same limitations on the numbers of visits, and the same lifetime dollar caps for psychiatric disorders as for all other medical disorders. In 2008, Congress passed the Mental Health Parity and Addiction Equity Act (Wellstone-Domenici Act). The act requires that the annual and lifetime limits of mental health benefits of any insurance plan be the same as for surgical or medical benefits. This was incorporated into President Barack Obama's health care reform efforts in 2010.[31] It sounds good, but there are loopholes: employers with fifty or fewer employees are exempt, employers can still purchase plans that limit the total number of visits per year, and employers don't have to obey this parity rule if it raises the health insurance cost to their business by more than 1 percent. Despite these loopholes, millions of people could benefit with expanded coverage and financial access to mental health treatment. As of the writing of this book, the future of this major health care reform legislation is politically uncertain. From the point of view of a psychiatrist though, it could be the most important step forward for people in need of mental health treatment in modern American history.

Surprisingly, if you are poor or disabled, the financial barriers to psychiatric treatment are sometimes fewer. The poor and the disabled have access to Medicaid and

Medicare, respectively. These two public insurance programs carry some of the most robust benefits for psychiatric treatment, especially in those states where these programs have not been given to managed care agencies. For example, the traditional Medicaid or Medicare policy has no limitation on the number of outpatient visits. Medicaid gives generous prescription benefits, and Medicare Part D now gives fairly good prescription coverage. And many states have a special pharmacy assistance program for those who are not poor enough to qualify for Medicaid, but fall into a certain "gray zone" where they are close to qualifying for Medicaid. This is particularly important in psychiatric care, since some of the most effective modern medications tend to be expensive.

The financial barriers to treatment are starting to break down. True parity of benefits for mental health treatment is growing. Though some coverage may be limited by the design of the policy or by heavy-handed managed care, clinical experience has taught me that *some* good and competent treatment is better than no treatment at all.

Regional Differences

Mental Health America looked at differences in the rates of depression across all fifty states from 2002 to 2006. The organization's rankings, published in 2007, are fascinating.[32] They show that the "mentally healthiest" state is South Dakota, and the "least healthiest" is Utah. This was determined based on rates of depression, rates of suicide, how commonly people experienced "serious psychological distress," and the number of "poor mental health days" respondents experienced in the past year. The organization found that mental health ratings were associated with a variety of regional factors. The findings were consistent with what you would expect. For example, the more mental health professionals a state had, the lower the suicide rate. Similarly, those states with a higher percentage of the population receiving mental health treatment had lower suicide rates. Also, the states where cost of treatment was reported to be a problem had poorer mental health. Rural people were less likely to get treatment than those in suburban areas. Lastly, the higher the state's average educational level, the better it ranked on mental health and use of mental health services. So, like other kinds of medical conditions, where people live influences their mental health and access to treatment for those kinds of problems. If it's hard to get, people are less willing to try it.

• • •

Now that you have gained some understanding of the reasons why the troubled person you are trying to help hasn't sought treatment on his or her own, you are now ready to learn what the actual treatment process entails, beginning with getting an evaluation.

4

The Goal of Helping: Getting an Evaluation

"The value of compassion cannot be over-emphasized . . .
No greater burden can be borne by an individual
than to know no one cares or understands."
— ARTHUR H. STAINBACK

You've decided that your loved one or friend is struggling with a mental or emotional problem that warrants professional attention. You have now learned possible reasons why he has not brought himself to a doctor or other mental health professional, putting you into the position to help him do so. You're prepared to step in and help, but what does that mean? What are you trying to achieve? In this chapter, you will learn in more detail about the goal—a proper evaluation by a mental health professional. That is the starting place for building a solution by figuring out what is going on, implementing a treatment plan, and moving toward healing and recovery. In the chapters that follow, you will be given a step-by-step plan for engaging your friend or loved one and convincing him or her to get help. The Seven Steps reference in the appendix of this book is a good summary of this process once you've learned about each step.

It All Starts with a Diagnosis

In the third century B.C., the Greek physician Hippocrates (recorded history's first physician, often called "the father of medicine") wrote, "Diagnosis is half the cure." Hippocrates recognized that the body malfunctions in characteristic ways and that any effective treatment must begin by discerning which known pattern of malfunctioning is happening. All treatment, physical or mental, begins with answering the question, What is going on here? The mind has characteristic ways that it malfunctions. As a helper, your primary goal is to get the person to consult with a mental health professional who can identify the problem and make a *diagnosis*.

Arriving at a diagnostic conclusion is helpful on two levels: diagnosis points to a relevant treatment approach, and determining what's wrong provides some comfort to the patient. The psychiatrist Daniel Carlat wrote in his 2010 book *Unhinged:*

> Providing patients with a diagnosis, which psychiatrists typically do at the end of the first visit, is a form of therapy. Part of what makes mental illness so painful is its terrible mystery. Patients in the midst of a crisis feel that they are spinning out of control, do not know what they are experiencing, and wonder if they will ever feel normal again. Providing them with an explanation goes a long way toward a cure.[33]

On the other hand, the word "diagnosis" in a *psychiatric* context can cause negative feelings. There is a concern that "labeling" is going on. Interestingly, there is more concern about labeling in psychiatry than in other medical fields. "Labeling" someone with diabetes, for instance, doesn't arouse worries of stereotyping the way that the diagnosis of schizophrenia does. This is further evidence of the stigma discussed in chapter 3.

All of medicine is a balancing act between treating a person as a unique individual while simultaneously looking for characteristic and recognizable patterns of how human beings malfunction. Identifying those patterns helps a care provider do the two things doctors have been asked to do since the time of Hippocrates: predict the future, and alter it. That is, provide a "prognosis" and "treatment," respectively. Good treatment recognizes the unique *individual* in the foreground, while keeping an eye on the *diagnosis* in the background. In this way, the balance between uniqueness and generalizations can be maintained to the advantage of the patient. We all take comfort in knowing that our "suffering" is a familiar one, has been seen in many others, and has been treated successfully. In fact, besides being of value in determining treatment, diagnosis can be a great value to the patient in opening the door to seeking support groups, research on the Internet, and news stories about emerging treatments.

How does a psychiatrist or psychologist make a diagnosis? In this age of technology, psychiatry remains one of the purest clinical specialties. The diagnostic tools of medicine for hundreds of years consisted of the doctor's verbal interview of the patient along with direct observation. In psychiatry, those remain the primary methods of determining what is going on with the person.

At Johns Hopkins Hospital, the "patron saint" of the medical institution was, and remains, Sir William Osler (1849–1919), who helped found the medical school. Osler was most famous for his diagnostic skills, developed before modern technology was available to assist in making medical diagnoses. He would sit and talk with a patient, taking a very careful history, asking myriad questions, and using the interview to chart the course of symptoms over time. He would watch the patient closely, paying attention to detail and noting the color of the skin, the shape of the head, the use of limbs while speaking, the pulses showing through the skin, muscle mass, the eyes, on and on. Finally, he would lay his hands on the patient (along with the newly developed stethoscope), examining the entire body. He would use his sense of smell, and even taste (e.g., a "sweet" urine suggested diabetes). True, these techniques had been used by physicians for centuries, but few had mastery as celebrated as William Osler's. To this day, a detailed history and physical examination are considered the main act of diagnosis, for which tests like CAT scans and lab work are used to *confirm* diagnostic hypotheses made during an exam.

Psychiatry relies largely on the "Oslerian" style, in which a detailed history and a "chair side" examination are the primary tools for making a diagnosis. There are no other technologies yet developed to "confirm" a psychiatric diagnosis—no imaging studies, no blood tests, no brain wave scans, not even a paper-and-pencil test, which can confirm a psychiatric diagnosis the way an EKG or blood test can confirm that a patient has had a heart attack. (Some psychiatric clinics may try to sell patients on extensive, and expensive, imaging tests as part of the evaluation to diagnose mental disorders. Beware those claims! There are currently *no* such tests that can be reliably used in this way.) However, like in other areas of medicine, psychiatric diagnosis is not an exact science. In Osler's own immortal words, "If it were not for the great variability among individuals, medicine would be a science, not an art."

In medicine, however, science shakes hands with art. Technology has become so relevant in other fields of medicine, it has virtually taken over the tradition of taking a health history and performing a physical examination as the gold standard. In cardiology, for example, you are diagnosed with having had a heart attack (a myocardial infarction) *only* if the EKG and blood tests say so, no matter what the history or physical exam might suggest. Not so in psychiatry. The gold standard remains diagnostic conclusions, based on established criteria, drawn from a psychiatric interview with the patient and often other informants. Tests can be used to rule out other diagnoses, such as a CT scan of the brain to make sure there isn't a brain tumor, or an EEG to make sure that the symptoms aren't being caused by a seizure. But ruling out other possibilities is a completely different matter than confirming a diagnosis.

A psychiatric or psychological evaluation is mostly a long interview. How long? It's not standardized, but it's commonly accepted that the interview will take a minimum of forty to forty-five minutes, often even longer. The interviewer needs to go over the entire history of symptoms from their start (which may have been many years ago) to the present. In psychiatry, symptoms are viewed within the context of a person's development, social life, family life, education, and vocation, which means that information needs to be collected as well. Then there are specialized questions to assess the present state of thinking, feelings, and behaviors and to explore the possibility of symptoms the patient may not have mentioned. Finally, if there has been any past treatment, it's useful to have a chance to examine and digest those records. In other words, the diagnosis takes time. It's not just a matter of simply saying "ah" while someone looks in your throat and feels your pulse. It may take a few visits, or involve diagnostic screening tests to rule out other possibilities.

After the diagnosis—after the question What's going on here? has been answered—the next step is determining what to do about it. Now, a treatment plan needs to be developed. Your major goal, convincing your friend or loved one to get help, has been met when a diagnosis has been made and a treatment course has been suggested.

Where to Start

To whom should you turn for a proper diagnosis? If at all possible, the best place to start is with a psychiatrist—the medical professional with the most comprehensive understanding of the human mind, brain, and body. Let me explain why.

Extensive training permits a psychiatrist to think through a multidimensional evaluation, including the possibility of medical illness, brain disease, social factors, and/or psychological and developmental issues. This is why a psychiatrist can prescribe the most comprehensive range of treatment options: psychotherapy in the office, prescription medication, couples therapy, family therapy, inpatient hospital treatment, emergency room evaluations, day programs, and residential treatment.

Psychiatrists are physicians who have gone to medical school and interned for a year in neurology and medicine, after which they train as residents in psychiatry for at least three more years, sometimes more. They are exposed to the broadest possible range of cases, from those who are merely stressed and troubled to the profoundly mentally ill. They train in outpatient offices and in hospitals, nursing homes, clinics, and other places. All psychiatrists receive this broad and deep training as their standard residency education. Other kinds of mental health professionals might have elected training in one or two of these areas, but not all. The one core service that all psychiatrists are trained to offer, however, is a *comprehensive initial evaluation*, which results in an answer (or answers) to that all-important question: What's going on here? That, in turn, leads to a variety of answers to the next question: What can be done to help? After the evaluation, the psychiatrist may continue to treat the individual or make a referral to a different kind of mental health professional, such as a social worker or psychologist. If a physical disorder is suspected as the underlying cause of the problem, there may be a referral to a different kind of medical specialist.

Seeing a psychiatrist first, however, is not always an option in every case. Psychiatrists may be few and far between, particularly outside of major metropolitan areas. It might take weeks to get an appointment in some cases where psychiatrists are in short supply. It takes longer to be seen by a psychiatrist in private practice than one who serves in a large clinic where the evaluation process is some-what briefer and more streamlined. Sometimes costs and co-pays are a factor; psychiatrists are, because of their train-ing as physicians, typically more expensive than psycholo-gists, social workers, psychiatric nurses, and other trained counselors.

A wide range of mental health professionals have some training in diagnostic evaluation. All have been taught that diagnosis is the first step to healing, and all are familiar with the broad variety of possible mental disorders. Non-psychiatrists (because they are not physicians) may not be as familiar with other medical conditions that can mimic psychiatric disorders, and they are less likely to have been exposed to people with the most severe mental illnesses in their training. However, they can collaborate with a patient's primary care physician or with psychiatrist colleagues to provide further diagnostic clarification and create a comprehensive treatment plan.

How to Find a Psychiatrist or Other Mental Health Professional

How do you find *any* doctor when you need one? The most common way is to get a referral from a doctor you already see, typically your primary care doctor. Most primary care doctors know at least one psychiatrist, just as they know at least one cardiologist. Some know other kinds of mental health counselors as well, including psychologists, social workers, or other therapists with whom they collaborate. Still, try to start with a psychiatrist, if at all possible.

When people called my radio show, I would ask if a medical school was within reasonable driving distance. Virtually every medical school has a department of psychiatry and treatment clinics. The other possible advantage is that many have clinics run by psychiatric residents in training, which often provide treatment for free or a minimal charge.

Another way to find a mental health professional is to ask anyone you know who has seen one, especially if the experience has been a positive one. Most insurance companies maintain a list of specialists who participate in their coverage plan, and a call to your insurance carrier can net you a referral to someone in your area. There is also the Internet. You will find some useful websites and tips about how to find psychiatrists and other mental health professionals in the resources section on pages 257–259.

Treatment Works!

During the initial evaluation the professional has an additional goal beyond reaching a diagnostic conclusion. If there is a problem that needs treatment, the skillful evaluator's job is to try and get the patient to agree to move forward with appropriate treatment. It's helpful to know something about psychiatric treatments that might follow that initial evaluation.

Contrary to conventional expectations, many people struggling with emotional and mental health issues have very treatable conditions. As a matter of fact, the success rates of treatments for mental health problems are incredibly high. According to the National Institute of Mental Health, treatment success rates are

- 85 percent for major depression
- 80 percent for panic disorder
- 80 percent for manic depression
- 60 percent for obsessive-compulsive disorder
- as high as 75 percent for schizophrenia[34]

These numbers are at least as high, if not higher, than the success rate of established treatments for many other common medical conditions such as diabetes, congestive heart failure, and angina.

In this context, "success" hearkens back to Freud's useful generalization about the manifestation of good mental health: "the ability to live and work effectively." That can mean preservation of a job or relationship, the ability to complete an education, the reversal of a medical condition that was neglected because of mental problems, the ability to travel without debilitating symptoms, even the preservation of life by preventing suicide.

Will Treatment Be Tolerable?

A caller to my radio show once asked, "If I *can* convince my father to see a psychiatrist, I predict that he won't like it and will have a bad experience. Is this a common way things go?" Happily, the answer is *no*. Actually, it's much more common for a person to have a positive experience with treatment. A *Consumer Reports* survey found that almost 90 percent of people who had consulted a mental health professional felt they were helped "somewhat" or "a lot." [35]

Basic Types of Treatment

Nowadays, some believe that all doctors want to do is "throw drugs" at mental health concerns. A middle-aged woman who called my show was struggling with her body image. She was so preoccupied with it that she was unable to enjoy other obvious blessings in her life. Yet she wasn't certain about seeking treatment; she was concerned that I might not listen to her or take the time to understand her problem, but rather "push pills" at her. Not only is this not my practice but also the *Consumer Reports* survey shows that only 3 percent of encounters with psychiatrists result in the prescription of drugs alone.

Psychiatric medications have been one of the most profound contributions to the treatment of emotional and behavioral problems, starting in the 1950s. It is not an understatement to call them "revolutionary." Most problems, however, can be treated without medications, but those problems that would benefit from medications benefit remarkably. Antidepressants, anti-anxiety medications, medications for attention deficit disorder, mood stabilizers, anti-psychotics, and other types of medications have literally helped save lives, jobs, marriages, and sanity. However, in medical school, where I learned many Latin phrases, one of my favorites was *nullum gratuitum prandium,* "There's no free lunch." That is, significant problems can require powerful medicines, and the flip side of efficacy is side effects. It's a balancing act that calls for skillful attention. So, medication needs to be administered with discernment, caution, and as much collaboration with a patient as feasible. The vast majority of patients are able to be partners in choice of medication, adjustment of doses, and response to side effects. Very rarely is a patient so impaired that medication needs to be administered in an emergency, in the hope of improving his or her mental state enough to become a more rational partner in the process.

All types of treatment, even careful medication prescribing, take time. Psychiatry may be one of the last specialties in medicine where the doctor takes a fair amount of time to explore a patient's suffering. Time is one of the essential therapeutic tools of the psychiatrist. Frankly, in our increasingly rushed and crowded lives, time remains one of the most important commodities any healer can provide. The vital component of time is so essential to mental health treatment that, unlike any other area of medicine, mental health professionals still promise a treatment session with a set amount of time whenever they meet a patient. Knowing how long each appointment will be helps both the patient and care provider pace themselves and sets expectations for a piece of work that can be accomplished. Treatment is never a single visit like, say, for a sore throat. It is a series of visits, sometimes limited, but they can be open ended as the goals of treatment may evolve with each step of improvement.

Treatment for an individual problem may consist of talk therapy, behavioral therapy, or medication, but most often a combination of all of these. Treatment will also depend on whether it's given in an outpatient or inpatient environment.

Outpatient Treatment

This is essentially *any* kind of treatment administered in an office setting. The office can be a stand-alone private practice or part of a larger clinic. Outpatient treatment involves regular appointments that usually last between twenty-five and sixty minutes (but which can be longer, especially for family or couples sessions). Usually, treatment starts with one to four sessions a month on average and then tapers off depending on the severity and nature of the condition.

What happens during these visits?

If the patient is taking medication, the doctor may ask about symptoms and any side effects of the medication. She may want to order laboratory tests, such as thyroid levels, medication blood levels, or liver function tests. She may make dosage adjustments or switch to a different medication, depending on response and side effects. The patient should be provided with education about the medication and the condition being treated, as well as have an opportunity to ask questions during the visit, much like a follow-up visit with a primary care physician or other medical specialist who is treating an illness or injury.

If the patient is also engaged in other forms of therapy, such as talk therapy, that might take up the majority of the visit. Sometimes, a person will see a psychiatrist for medication, and a non-psychiatrist therapist for other treatments. It's not unusual to have *two* care providers—a psychiatrist and a counselor/therapist. Some psychiatrists, like myself, provide both kinds of treatments.

Most therapy treatments involve engaging in conversations. Those conversations between patient and therapist are largely dialogues that focus on the patient's life. Usually, these conversations are guided by the therapist according to the psychological principles of his or her particular practice. Certain specialized forms of therapy may involve *doing* something. Treatment for elevator phobias, for example, might involve working with an actual elevator in a systematic way. Treatment for fear of germs might involve a systematic exposure to dirty surfaces and learning to tolerate the anxiety. These *doing* therapies are called "behavioral therapies."

Some therapy sessions are done within a group comprised of people who share related problems. In group therapy, the professional therapist not only gives feedback to each individual but also facilitates cross-talk between members of the group who, in turn, support each other with the help of the professional leader. Therapy sessions can also involve a facilitated conversation between the patient and a significant other.

Inpatient Treatment

This generally refers to treatment within a hospital setting. Inpatient treatment could take place in a psychiatric unit of a general hospital or in a specialty hospital that treats psychiatric problems only. Either way, it usually involves checking into a hospital for a number of days. Treatment in modern hospitals is mostly done with group therapies throughout the day in addition to a daily private meeting with the doctor and other members of the treatment team, including a nurse and social worker (who also meet with a patient's family). Medication is common, but not a universal part of a hospital stay, and very rarely other treatments are given, such as electroconvulsive therapy (an extremely effective treatment that is still frequently used, voluntarily).

Unlike outpatient settings, inpatient treatment can also accommodate people who are there involuntarily (an approach we will explore in detail in chapter 9). This fact, combined with the practice of health insurance companies to preauthorize treatment (i.e., decide if inpatient treatment is necessary), means that modern psychiatric hospitalization tends to be reserved for people who are seriously ill, especially compared to decades past. It is not unusual for a patient to make a transition to a *day* hospital (also called "partial" hospital) as he or she recovers. This is similar to a hospital, but patients get to go home every night and on weekends.

• • •

Right now, you do not need to ponder what kind of treatment your friend might need or in which setting that treatment will be given. Your role is to appreciate the importance of guiding him or her to a professional who can make a diagnosis and determine the best treatment plan. Now that you know what you are trying to achieve, your next task is to find the right time and place to start the conversation.

5

How to Choose the Right Time and Place

*"To everything there is a season, and
a time to every purpose under heaven."*

— ECCLESIASTES 3:1

Timing Is (Almost) Everything

You are ready to talk to your friend or relative about the benefit of getting help. Good! But you must first consider when and where to broach the subject. Timing is critical when undertaking such a delicate conversation. This topic is a highly volatile one, and your timing needs to respect that. The best way I can advise you about how to time your approach is to let you learn from the mistakes in timing I have seen over the years. There aren't so much *right* times as *wrong* times to ask, "Can we talk?"

Not Now

Here are a few of the times and situations when you should avoid starting this sensitive conversation, if at all possible.

Potentially Defensive Times

Be aware of when that person might be in a particularly defensive state. Defenses are lowest first thing in the morning and again when we wind down to go to sleep at night. Defenses are highest under the pressure of a deadline, when in a rush, during a confrontational argument, when being criticized, and if awakened in the middle of the night. Interestingly, when someone is intoxicated, *inhibitions* may drop but *defenses* may rise—and in an exaggerated way (an instinctual attempt to protect one's self in the state of decreased inhibitions).

Family Gatherings

Launching into a well-intended conversation about the behavior that needs attention is best avoided during family gatherings. Birthdays, celebrations, holidays, or events such as weddings, funerals, christenings, or bar mitzvahs are *not* the time to ask, "Can we talk?" Even in the happiest families, these times can be tense. When families get together, people want to look "okay" to other family members. There is often a little showing off going on, especially between siblings and in front of their parents. Raising problems at these times—even in a private setting—can be deeply upsetting and embarrassing. And turning the attention away from the purpose of the occasion can poison the memory of the event for years to come. Don't do it.

As you may know from experience, it is not uncommon for emotions to go off "into left field" at family functions for any number of reasons. Drinking, fighting, the rehashing of old issues—all can and do occur during the stress of family gatherings. Certain problems are glaringly obvious, and it can be difficult to resist confronting the issues right then and there. But, unless there is a life-threatening emergency involving someone's behavior, *hold back!* You will be seen as confrontational, and you want to stay away from that posture if you can. (The exceptions are addressed in chapter 9.) Confrontation feels adversarial. I have seen many disastrous results when well-meaning people feel the need to address problems during family gatherings. What had been intended as caring comes out as provocative, escalates to a confrontation, and kindles into a raging family bonfire. At that point, you will have a lot more damage to repair.

The bottom line is this: if, during a family gathering, you become aware of a loved one's emotional distress and think there might be a possible psychiatric problem, make a mental note of it, file it away, and make plans to find a more private, less emotionally charged time and place to approach the troubled person. This may be particularly difficult because these days families often live long distances apart; the most *convenient* time to address a problem is when everyone is together for an event. *Avoid the temptation.* It is better to speak with a family member later, during a calm time— even if it is over the *phone*—than it is to speak face-to-face, during a family gathering for a holiday or important event.

When Arguing or Right After

Your concern about a loved one's mental health is not something to bring up when arguing or fighting. Nor is it something to tack on at the end of a discussion about another matter. The *amygdala* is the part of the brain that gets fired up when we are mad or scared. It's the so-called fight-or-flight center in the brain. An argument is settled in a different part of the brain, the reasoning frontal lobe. The amygdala keeps firing for a while even after an argument is settled. So, when you think it's over and you can talk about more general issues, like the other's mental health, that amygdala is still chirping away, making the mind un-receptive, emotional, and self-protective. It's still in fight-or-flight mode. So, not only in the midst of a fight, but also in the hours after a fight, approaching the other to talk about your mental health concerns is ill-advised. Moreover, it might be viewed by the other as just an attempt to invali-date his argument, trumping him by asserting that he might have a psychiatric problem.

• CAROL AND BOB •

Carol and Bob have just argued about Carol's leaving dirty dishes in the sink:

Bob: *So, I'm sorry I yelled at you.*

Carol: *All right, I'll try to wash the dishes sooner after I eat. I get that it bugs you to leave them sitting dirty in the sink.*

Bob: *I think "bug" is an understatement.*

Carol: *I know. In fact, you can sometimes get pretty out there about cleanliness, and it seems to be getting worse. Frankly, I've been meaning to talk to you about that: the way you get crazy about cleaning. I've seen you spend a huge amount of time clean-ing the sink and counters, going over and over them. You have started to spend an incredible amount of time in the bathroom and I hear the water running in the sink for a long time.*

Bob: *So?*

Carol: *And I've seen you doing this thing where you go over to the stove at least ten times to check*

> *repeatedly that it's shut off. You arrange the boxes in the pantry over and over, to get them in just the right order of sizes from lowest to highest, and you get irritated when I don't pay attention to that order when I put the cereal back in the pantry.*

Bob: *(starting to yell) We were talking about the dirty dishes in the sink; now you're changing the subject!*

Carol: *But that is the subject—your neat-freak stuff is getting out of hand.*

Bob: *What, now you're saying I'm crazy?*

Carol: *No, that's not . . .*

Bob: *So, I tell you that you should wash the dishes a bit sooner, and now you're saying that something is wrong with me for asking for that? Okay, now it's MY problem, huh? Nothing wrong with you then? It's not you who maybe has a mental problem with being a slob?!*

And they have fallen down the well, back into arguing. Now the argument is no longer about whether dishes should be cleaned sooner rather than later. It's about who has the "mental problem." Carol should have waited until at least the day after the argument and Bob would have been more receptive.

When Drinking

Intoxicants like alcohol—even at very mild levels—can alter emotional responses, memory, and receptivity. Even a little bit of drinking should cause you to postpone your conversation. You might think that people are less defensive and more open when drinking. This can be true. Clinical experience has shown, however, that this kind of defenses-down openness is not *sustainable* and does not endure after sobering up. If someone seems open when drunk, he or she will close up again when sober. And, even in the case of very mild intoxicant levels, there may be trouble later remembering what was discussed. If the drinker insists he or she is unaffected and "perfectly sober," don't buy it! As someone with an important and delicate mission, *wait*.

By E-mail or Text

It might be tempting to use e-mail to start the conversation with your friend, because it feels easier and less emotionally intense or confrontational than speaking face-to-face. We have come to think of e-mail as a way to communicate outside the stream of time: you write it when convenient and the recipient reads it when convenient. Actually, an e-mail note is much more likely to be misinterpreted than a face-to-face conversation, and you have far less control over the message. The recipient can read it at any time—including when upset about something else, when intoxicated, when fatigued, when suffering from lack of sleep, etc. In people under age thirty, texting has become an increasingly dominant form of communication. This is even worse than e-mail for addressing serious concerns. It is far too brief, abbreviated, and also easily discoverable by others (most phones are not password protected, like e-mail).

I strongly recommend against e-mail or texting approaches beyond the simplest of messages like, "I need to talk to you about something important. When can we get together?" E-mail and texting have been a part of my patients' lives now for some years. You might think this particular recommendation that texting be limited to a brief invitation is common sense. It amazes me how often people initiate and pursue some very serious topics in a stream of text messages. Patients will actually show me those texts in the course of therapy. As a psychiatrist, I have learned how vulnerable both e-mail and texts are to misinterpretation, and the tendency for the recipient to read between the lines (often inaccurately). When patients have shown me these writings, I sometimes have markedly different interpretations of what I am reading than they have.

If you can't meet in person because of distance, the phone is preferable to e-mail. In a phone conversation, the nuance of voice can often convey subtleties like compassion. Also, any misinterpretations of your words can quickly be corrected in the moment, something that cannot be done with e-mail exchanges. Video conferencing approaches such as Skype™ are even better than phone calls because body language is important in building a sense of safety in the face of vulnerability, and allows a visual modality to complement the words. Also, it's done in real time, like a phone call.

Prepare the Way: The Power of Anticipation

This conversation deserves to be labeled as "special," and choosing the right time and place reinforces that. To this end, it is good to have the other person anticipate some kind of serious and meaningful conversation. People do better when they can prepare themselves for a serious talk rather than being blindsided by a sudden approach. You don't have to say *what* you want to talk about, just that you want to talk. If you do not say what the topic is, your friend will not be as likely to prepare a defense, but be more ready to hear something serious. He or she might be worried, but that's okay. Worry is a sign of caring, and that's precisely why you are the right person to initiate this talk. Here's an example of what I mean:

Carol: *I'd like to sit down together for twenty minutes after work tomorrow and talk with you about something important.*

Bob: *You're scaring me. What's it about?*

Carol: *Don't worry, nothing to be scared about. It's something I really care about, and want to discuss it with you, but we need the time and focus to do it, rather than talking about it off-the-cuff right now. Okay?*

Bob: *Okay, but can you tell me what it's about now?*

Carol: *Don't be worried, just know that I want to discuss something. It's not something I'm angry about, or any big surprise or catastrophe I'm going to spring on you. Like I said, it's important enough that we need to focus on it and we'll do that in person, together, tomorrow. I want to think more about how to best discuss it. How about we plan to sit down when I get home from work to talk?*

Carol gets Bob to anticipate that something of importance is coming, probably serious. She creates his anticipation by putting it off, dressing it in the language of importance, explaining that it is significant enough for her to carefully get her thoughts together to talk about it. That suggests she has been thinking about this for a while, that it's a delicate matter, and that she wants to get it right. Bob can infer that she is trying to present something in a way that is diplomatic, sensitive to the fact that it may be a difficult conversation. Carol tries to reassure Bob that it's nothing to be afraid of, that he isn't going to be scolded or at the receiving end of anger. Nor will it be some huge news that could mean major consequences that will disrupt the family, like being fired or diagnosed with a terrible disease. This isn't an impulsive blurting; it's a planned strategic campaign. If you are a very impulsive person, a person who can't hold back for a while, or if your "Bob" is good at needling you until you come out with it, maybe you should not approach things in this way.

Take a note from the professional's power of establishing a special time when approaching the person you are trying to help. Mental health providers use this tool in treatment. It's built into every form of mental health treatment: an appointment. In fact, all healers, whether medical or psychiatric, conventional or alternative, work via a pre-arranged and periodic appointment time. This is not merely a convenience; it's one of the medically active ingredients in what we do. The great scientist of psychotherapy, Jerome Frank, in his book *Persuasion and Healing*, showed that this approach to time is one of the common ingredients in almost all of the nearly three hundred different named types of psychotherapy. It is very much part of how all these various methods work as well. They all establish a special time in which a person's problem gets to be the center of attention.

Therapists have come to refer to this special time and place with a poetic term—a vessel. Patients enter into and exit the vessel and, in between those two gestures, the place and time are all theirs. A fixed appointment duration of twenty-five or fifty minutes is an important part of the process. Patients know in advance how much time they have, and they and the psychiatrist can work together to pace things to fit into that time. This allows a different, potentially deeper level of communication than the unspecified amount of time patients have with other kinds of doctors.

So, even if you don't prepare the way with anticipation, like Carol did with Bob, consider beginning simply with the invitation for a special meeting, appointment, outing, or get-together. Perhaps, the first time, you'll have no other agenda or purpose than to listen actively, inquire about the other's interior emotional life, and show that you care and want to help.

There's a Place for Us

You must also find the right location for this conversation. You'll need to select a place that is comfortable and emotionally neutral. It should also be a place where phone calls, doorbells, children, neighbors, or colleagues will not interrupt you. A place where you can focus, free of distractions, and unassociated with previous traumas or highly emotional experiences is best. The space can be indoors or outdoors, but it should be a place where you both can be comfortable, and able to linger as long as you need to.

You might think it should always be a strictly private place. That may sometimes not be the best choice. Some of the people with whom I have worked chose a more public place, where others are around, but where conversations cannot be easily overheard. A public park or busy restaurant might have advantages. Most people are more behaviorally restrained, civil, or appropriate when in a public place around strangers. If the person is volatile, verbally abusive, or prone to tantrums, those behaviors are less likely in, say, a crowded restaurant in a private booth. Also, the other can feel less "trapped" or less like a "captive audience" in a public place. If worse comes to worst, he or she can get up and leave. That may be harder to do in a home or car.

Anticipate the Other Person's Taking Offense, Feeling Hurt

• MICHAEL •

Michael came to me about the effect his father's alcoholism had on him. He explained his fears: "If I tell him that I think he has a drinking problem and that it has had a negative impact on me, it will hurt him. It would be unkind." When we talked about it further, he revealed that he was afraid that, at best, his father would feel bad if told he had a problem, and that, at worst, he would get very angry; either way it would seriously wound their relationship.

I pointed out that their relationship was already damaged by the father's drinking problem. This damage was happening "in secret" (it was something nobody was talking about), but it was real. We examined whether bringing an already damaging problem into the light would create more harm, and if that additional pain would be permanent or only temporary on the way to repairing things. This shift in perspective turned out to be all Michael needed to start the conversation with his father. Sometimes the key accomplishment in mental health treatment is nothing more or less than a shift in perspective.

One of the reactions that so many helpers fear is that the other will say, "I'm not crazy!" Fear of offending or angering the person who needs psychiatric help is probably the greatest barrier to action on the part of those who are concerned. A person can feel devalued (or insulted) when told that psychiatric evaluation and treatment might be in order. This can be interpreted as being called *crazy, stupid, unfit,* or *incompetent.* (One of the best book titles ever is a popular book on adult attention deficit disorder, *You Mean I'm Not Lazy, Stupid or Crazy?* by Kate Kelly and Peggy Ramundo.) The old, disparaging joke is, "You have to be crazy to see a psychiatrist!" There is a tendency to associate mental health therapists, particularly psychiatrists, with treating "craziness." Of course, these are stereotypes and stigmas, as discussed in chapter 3, but they need to be anticipated.

Being told that you might have a psychiatric problem can hurt. It can hurt more than having someone point out, say, a suspicious-looking mole that ought to be examined by a dermatologist. But this should not be surprising. To hear someone we trust say that there is a problem with our thoughts, feelings, or behaviors can be crushing. We can be left feeling vulnerable, helpless, frightened, and embarrassed.

A woman who was worried about her husband's angry, explosive outbursts told me she was terrified of upsetting him by asking if he would consider getting help. She was thinking of calling his family doctor (see chapter 7). Sometimes it's easy to miss the obvious. I pointed out that she was *already living with* the angry outbursts. Thinking about it, she concluded that this was true and that they probably wouldn't get any worse if she asked him to get a medical evaluation for that behavior. "You're right, it's already bad enough." Of course, sometimes violence is a reality. Prior violent behavior is the best predictor that your loved one could act violently when approaching him or her about getting psychological help. If that describes your situation, it's best to be sure that you have someone with you (chapter 7) or, if violence seems very likely, make use of the civil authorities to get the person help, as described in chapter 9.

One of the most common psychological defenses we have when we are afraid is anger. Feeling that you've been insulted is actually a form of fear. It is vitally important to understand this as you make your approach. Use caution and sensitivity, and be prepared for a possible angry response. This reaction—*you are being insulting!*—is (ironically) a sign that you are on the right track. There *is* a problem and you have gotten close to it.

It is key to your success that you approach the disturbed person with an understanding that this might feel unkind. Disarming that expectation can be helpful; head off such a reaction by voicing your anticipation of hurt feelings and your reassurance that is not your intention at all, that you are acting out of love or concern, and that you think getting professional help will make the other feel better. Moreover, if your approach heavily focuses on *your* feelings—how this problem/behavior is affecting you or others—you will be received as far less critical. It's easier to criticize and invalidate facts than feelings. So bringing out your own feelings about the problem softens the possible experience of hurt and shame in the other. This gives you a chance to avoid the defensive denial or anger that makes you out to be the "bad guy" for voicing concern and bringing the problem into the light of day. One effective way I have seen people head off the "I'm not crazy" response is for the helper to say, "No, you're not, but your behavior is actually starting to make *me* feel that way. I am suffering, our relationship is suffering, and that's why I am talking to you about this." Remember, the whole reason you are eligible to make the approach is because you have a relationship with this person. So, how you feel is not irrelevant or totally insignificant to the other. We'll return to the power of your relationship in the next few chapters.

In the next chapter, you will find tips on how to use non-shaming, minimally threatening language. This will help as you make the first approach, the opening pitch, to talk about your concerns and, ultimately, lead your friend or loved one to the help he or she needs.

6

How to Make Your Approach

"When people are preparing a telegram, notice how carefully they consider each word before they put it down. That is how careful we must be when we speak."

— ISRAEL MEIR KAGAN

Visualize Building a Bridge

The goal of this book is to help you accomplish one thing: getting someone you care about to agree to a psychiatric evaluation. To start, you might visualize a bridge that stretches between how things are now and the goal of a psychiatric consultation. You must convince the other to walk across that bridge with you. To cross that bridge together, you need to start on the same side. The person you are trying to help is not a stranger. You already have a connection. You care and want to help. The difficulty of this task will depend on the degree of insight and awareness the other has regarding the mental problem.

As discussed in chapter 3, it is not unusual for a troubled person to be unwilling or even unable to observe himself or herself objectively. This can present a real barrier—to be successful you need to start with mutual agreement that there *is* a problem. Your first goal may be to get the person to acknowledge that she may be in some kind of emotional trouble. To achieve your goal, you will need to use basic principles of negotiation.

The starting point is trying to establish that you and the other are *on the same side.* You are both looking at a similar goal: a better business relationship, a happier marriage, less suffering for the other (and maybe for you, too), an improved personal relationship, more independent functioning, and so on. This isn't a business negotiation with conflicting interests on each side. You are on the same side. But what if you encounter resistance?

One of the best ways to get through the resistance is to make a genuine effort to *listen* to what the other is feeling. This goes way beyond the usual perfunctory, "How are you?" to which most people reflexively answer: "Fine." In *Persuasion and Healing,* Jerome Frank points out that listening in a non-threatening way and taking another person's suffering seriously, giving the person the feeling that his or her emotions are *visible* to you, are features common to the different kinds of professional psychotherapy (and there are hundreds) and other related healing techniques. As a matter of fact, this is one of the most basic skills new physician residents learn on the path to becoming psychiatrists—how to listen seriously.

Amazing as it might seem, for some individuals a psychiatrist is the first person who has ever really listened, asked deeper questions about feelings, and not only allowed but also welcomed full responses. Carl Rogers, the great psychotherapist, noted that this kind of listening (and the underlying openness in the listener), which he called "unconditional positive regard," was probably key to how psychotherapy helps people change. This can produce very positive and receptive feelings in the person to whom you are listening. One of the best compliments that people tend to give out is, "She is a great listener." Those are the people we often remember the most fondly since, as Maya Angelou said, "People will forget what you said, people will forget what you did, but people will never forget how you made them feel."

Of course, listening is not *all* there is to psychiatric treatment, but it's a vital foundation. I compare it to a sterile field in surgery. There is much more to a good surgical operation than having a sterile field in which to operate, but without this foundation it's unlikely that the outcome of the surgery will be optimal.

In his bestselling book, *Getting Past No*, negotiation guru William Ury offers tips for overcoming objections to your argument or desire. He believes that building a bridge to the other side is an absolutely essential part of negotiating agreements. He writes an entire chapter entitled "Step to Their Side," which includes these strategies:

- Listen actively
- Give the other side a hearing
- Acknowledge the person's feelings
- Tune into the person's wavelength
- Acknowledge the person

These are all variations on the same theme: be receptive and receive the other through listening. This is a powerful tool for the task you have at hand.

Active Listening and Psychological Visibility

It is important to show the other person that you are, indeed, hearing him. This is done not only by being quiet and saying

little but also by reflecting back what you have heard, sometimes repeating what you hear, with only slight modifica-
tions. This is what's known as *active listening* (also referred
to as "emphatic reflectives")—making statements that mirror
what you have heard.

• GEORGE •

George: *I am sick of the way Mom treats me like a child.*

Sister: *You don't like how Mom is treating you.*

George: *That's right! It's almost like she doesn't trust me.*

Sister: *You feel untrusted.*

George: *Yeah, like she always knows better what's right for me than I do.*

Sister: *It's clear that you feel bad about that.*

George: *You know what I'm saying?*

Sister: *Uh huh, I do.*

Notice how George's sister is echoing what she hears,
always with the intention of letting him know she's getting
it, and particularly getting what it *feels like* to be in George's
shoes. She is empathizing even while demonstrating that
she is listening. George picks up on this when he says,
"You know what I'm saying," which is half statement, half
question. His sister replies simply, affirming that she does,
"I do." Getting your relative/friend/colleague to know that
you "get" what it feels like to be him, allows that person to
feel *psychologically visible.*

I cannot emphasize enough the importance of psychological visibility in this process. This idea was originally
articulated by Nathaniel Branden, the renowned psycholo-

gist of self-esteem, in his book *Honoring the Self*. He looked at the basic parenting tasks that go into building a child's self-esteem. He believed that a key psychological purpose of the parent–child relationship is to make a child sense that what she feels, thinks, and believes is acknowledged rather than ignored, minimized, or contradicted. He called this "psychological visibility." In a culture as harried as ours, that does not readily honor the inner voice but floods us with external stimulation, children and adults can easily become psychologically invisible to others and to themselves. Feeling psychologically invisible is probably one of the most common experiences of the patients I see—independent of the specific problems for which they are consulting me. Whether the underlying issue is psychosis, marriage problems, temper outbursts, depression, or substance abuse, this "invisibility" is an amazingly widespread feeling. This is why active listening, as George's sister is trying to do, is so effective in convincing the troubled person that you are on his side. It makes that person feel psychologically visible.

In my years of clinical work, I have come to the conclusion that some of the stigma people feel about coming for psychiatric help is due to a collective social collusion that (probably unintentionally) maintains psychological invisibility as a norm. The family and the social silence that so often accompanies emotional distress and mental illness keep the inner world invisible.

There are certain acceptable ways of making one's inner world visible: through dreams, art and literature, and some forms of religious experience. When the inner world is painful, these expressions can show up as nightmares, "visionary art," or religious agony. Some of these expressions are helpful ways to process mental pain. Though not always an effective alternative to treatment, these expressions are sometimes more socially acceptable than consulting a psychiatrist. To come to a psychiatrist means making the inside world of one's mental life visible to somebody else. In your efforts to help by providing active and non-judgmental listening, you offer an easier first step for the suffering one. And because you are not a stranger, you set the stage for the process to be successful.

This fact—that you are not a stranger—is a very real advantage that you have over any mental health professional. Being made to feel psychologically visible by someone who already knows you enacts an ideal parent–child situation, providing one of the core essences of such a relationship, according to Branden. In this sense, the relationship can feel very satisfying.

Make the Other Feel Safe

Some people have been so profoundly damaged in their early trust-building years of life, made to feel invisible, that the offer of visibility is scorned because it doesn't feel safe. In childhood, they may have experienced adult figures who should have been trustworthy but who were masquerading while intending to satisfy their own needs. These are the trickiest cases because these individuals will interpret your attempts to help them as threats. These are the people for whom a sense of safety is critical.

Certain psychiatric conditions, like paranoia, by the very nature of the pathology, *reinforce* invisibility. Indeed, paranoia seeks to preserve invisibility at all costs. The condition involves a fundamental breakdown in the apparatus that the mind uses to make bridges and connections to others, sometimes damaged by brain diseases, such as schizophrenia and autism, or occasionally broken from early life trauma.

You do not have to become a therapist to draft someone into a psychiatrist consultation. But you can borrow some of the language professionals use and thus establish yourself as being on the same side; you are a non-threatening ally who wants to help. Here are examples of ways to start the conversation and promote a sense of safety. They are taken from my own medical practice:

- "I am really interested in how you are feeling; tell me."
- "You seem down, or blue; tell me how you feel."
- "What's on your mind? Please talk to me, I'll listen."
- "I'd like to understand."
- "You seem to be in some pain; would you like to talk about it?"
- "Why do you think you are not eating [not sleeping, not getting up in the morning, not able to concentrate, losing weight, so often angry, crying so often, etc.]?"
- "What are your tears about?" (This is one of my standard questions when someone is crying in my office.)
- "You seem to not be feeling [sleeping, concentrating, eating, etc.] well. How *do* you feel?"
- "I'd like to listen to how you are feeling."
- "How are you? Really how ARE you? I have some time to listen."
- "I know it's hard, but can you put your feelings into words?"
- "What are your worries?"

- "Do you have some worries about yourself that you'd be willing to share with me? Maybe I can help."

Don't Avoid Signs of Suicidal Thoughts—
It Can't Hurt to Ask

When medical students first encounter psychiatry training they often fear asking people if they are having thoughts of harming themselves or taking their own lives. Students worry that asking the question might plant the idea in a person's mind that had not been there before. The students learn, however, that there is no evidence that this is the case. Coming from someone in a helping position, such questions can effectively *reveal* such feelings, not *produce* them.

I want to reassure you that it is important not to be scared of this topic. In fact, opening it up can be life saving. It can be the key point that gives you more leverage when trying to convince the person you are concerned about that it is time to get professional help. In my experience, the first time a person voices suicidal thoughts or plans may be when someone asks him or her directly. Hearing one's self actually speak about such feelings to a caring listener can shift their significance to a much higher level than just thinking about them, or even writing about them. It's not uncommon to avoid looking at the rise of such feelings in one's self by minimizing or denying them. More than once I have heard a patient who is verbalizing suicidal feelings for the first time say something like, "Oh my. I can't believe I'm feeling this way. Things are more serious than I realized."

Open up the topic of suicidal thoughts and feelings if the person you are trying to help is

- more sad or depressed than usual
- feeling hopeless
- speaking unusually negatively about herself

- saying things like "I don't know if I can go on,"
  "It's not worth it," "I can't take it anymore,"
  "People would be better off without me," or other
  statements that she may be ready to give up

Some of the questions professionals use to explore suicidal thinking are quite straightforward. You can use them, too. Here are some examples:

- Have you been having any thoughts of hurting yourself?
- Do you ever wish you wouldn't wake up in the morning?
- Have you been wanting to die?
- Have you given away any of your possessions to friends or loved ones because you think you won't be needing them anymore?
- Have you done any research about how to end your life?
- Have you been making any plans to hurt yourself?
- How far along are you in putting those plans into place?
- Have you written any "good-bye" notes?

If the answer to any of these or similar questions is "yes," this can be an opportunity for more direct engagement and support. Feedback like, "I am so grateful you shared these feelings with me; it's so important," can create a stronger sense of trust in you as a helper. You can then use this information to empower your urging for a mental health evaluation. For example, uncovering suicidal thinking can be fuel for the "please do it for me" approach (e.g.: "I'm really worried/scared that you are already having some thoughts like this. Please *help me* know that you are going to be safe and can get some help to turn this around."). In more urgent situations (as described in chapter 9), this information can be crucial if you have to take a more hardball approach and mobilize the involuntary treatment system.

It is important that you take any signs of suicidal thinking seriously. For more information, visit the website for the National Suicide Prevention Lifeline at www.suicide preventionlifeline.org. If you can't convince your loved one to get immediate help, provide him or her with the Lifeline's phone number (1-800-273-TALK) and encourage him or her to call if he or she is ever feeling desperate and can't talk to you about it.

How to Be Helpful to Someone Who Is Threatening Suicide

- Be direct. Talk openly and matter-of-factly about suicide.

- Be willing to listen. Allow expressions of feelings. Accept the feelings.

- Be non-judgmental. Don't debate whether suicide is right or wrong, or whether feelings are good or bad. Don't lecture on the value of life.

- Get involved. Become available. Show interest and support.

- Don't dare him or her to do it.

- Don't act shocked. This will put distance between you.

- Don't be sworn to secrecy. Seek support.

- Offer hope that alternatives are available but do not offer glib reassurance.

- Take action. Remove means, such as guns or stockpiled pills.

- Get help from persons or agencies specializing in crisis intervention and suicide prevention.

Source: National Suicide Prevention Lifeline

Tolerate Anger

A must for listening seriously is tolerating the other person's anger. This may be the hardest skill of all. Anger, especially when it comes from a loved one, shuts down our desire to listen. Yet, this is one of the most important things you can offer—an ability to stay in the listening position even in the face of anger. It's one of the main things that therapists offer. *Staying open to listening, even when the other is angry, is an excellent starting point for communicating with someone in distress.* This can be an important pillar in the bridge you are trying to build, a bridge to a psychiatric evaluation.

• **MARIA AND JAVIER** •

Maria: *I am furious with my boss. He is such a jerk. I think he hates me, and it makes me hate him, too. It makes me so angry just to talk about it.*

Javier: *I appreciate that you're angry, it's okay. Why are you so angry?*

Maria: *I don't know, but I am and I shouldn't be.*

Javier: *It's what you're feeling.*

Maria: *Let me tell you, I don't have a clue how to be at work when I'm so angry.*

Javier doesn't deny the anger or share the anger, but gives it space, gives permission for Maria to have whatever feeling she is feeling, right when she wants to shut herself down and forbid herself the anger: "I shouldn't be." When Javier gives her a path to voice the anger, it enables her to go on to talk about her helplessness in the face of that feeling. Maria is willing to talk about her helplessness because Javier didn't shut her down by saying something like, "You shouldn't be so angry." It's tempting to think you are helping by telling an angry person to not be angry, as if she could just shut it off because you advise it. This is not helpful, and it actually invalidates the feeling. Your advice may simply come from your discomfort with the other's anger.

One helpful tool when listening to anger is visualization, which I myself use in my work. Imagine a Plexiglas screen between you and the other. You can see, hear, and understand everything the other is saying, but the emotional energy cannot penetrate the screen. It stays on the other side; it belongs to the speaker and cannot come through the barrier to hit you. This visual image is just enough to remind me to detach, and to remember that the emotions do not belong to me and do not have to penetrate me.

Don't Go Away

You may be met with resistance, suspicion, or an attempt to shut the door by minimizing your questions or responding to them in a superficial or sarcastic response. In this case, you may need to press (but gently).

• STACY AND ANN •

Ann: *What is going on with you?*

Stacy: *I have to go pick up another package of diapers for the twins.*

Ann: *I'm asking you something different. I mean how are you—inside? What are you experiencing? You seem down, and haven't been eating much, have you noticed that?*

Stacy: *I'm fine.*

Ann: *You know I really am serious. I know you want to tell me that you're fine, but you don't have to.*

> *I really care about you, and I've noticed that*
> *you are crying a lot, and I hope you will talk to*
> *me about that, because I want to listen.*

Stacy: *It's nothing really.*

Ann: *Stacy, I wouldn't keep trying to talk about this*
if I didn't care or if I wasn't concerned. Ever
since the twins were born you haven't been
eating much, you talk negatively about yourself,
even though it's obvious to me that you're a
good mother. You don't laugh as easily as you
used to. You seem to be in pain, and I want you
to feel comfortable talking about that to me.

Stacy: *(starting to cry) I'm so ashamed of myself. I*
should feel so happy about the twins being
born, but I just can't feel that way, though I
try so hard to.

Ann: *I'm listening . . .*

Ann is intent on opening a door to Stacy's interior, and persists gently but firmly against Stacy's reflexive/defensive attempts to shut it. She won't have her queries brushed off with superficial responses. She won't go away. She makes observations that demonstrate the cause of her concern, and asks if Stacy has noticed these things about herself. Ann emphasizes a few times that she is coming from a caring position and that she is *sincere* ("I'm serious"). She calls attention to the level of seriousness by using Stacy's name directly in the dialogue (something that people on very familiar terms often do not do, and it gets one's attention). She shows that she wants to engage in active, non-judgmental listening by saying "talk about that *to* me," not "*with* me."

Ann's persistence is really important. Sticking with

it is key. That stick-to-itiveness may actually take place over a series of conversations, if the first few don't go far.

> **Ann:** *Stacy, I wouldn't continue to try to talk about this if I didn't care or if I wasn't concerned . . .*
>
> **Stacy:** *(interrupts) I don't want to talk about it now.*
>
> **Ann:** *That's fine. I'll ask you how you feel later. If you want to talk about it later, I'll be ready. Otherwise, I'll find another time to approach you. I'm not going away. I'm here when you're ready. I hope you'll come to me, but if not, I'll keep trying.*

The next day:

> **Ann:** *Remember the questions I asked about how you were doing yesterday?*
>
> **Stacy:** *Uh-huh.*
>
> **Ann:** *I'd like to ask you again now, since you weren't ready to talk yesterday. Are you ready now?*

And so on. Ann doesn't take no for an answer. The most common mistake people make in this process is giving up too early. Dealing with your own discouragement is vital. Remember, you may be *it*; the only person willing or able to do this.

In situations that aren't urgent or dangerous, if you have made your pitch and see that the other is not ready, find a way to keep the door open, and revisit it periodically, maybe letting a little time pass, perhaps a few weeks. Don't forget to come back, though.

> **Ann:** *Have you given any more thought to the idea I raised when I called you last month, about*

> *seeing someone who might be able to help you*
> *with your depression? I'm still concerned, and*
> *I know there is a lot they can do to help that*
> *these days.*

Stacy: *Leave me alone about that!*

Ann: *It's hard to leave you alone about it when you*
seem to be having such a hard time. Maybe I'll
just send you something to read about depres-
sion, and ask you again if you're ready, next time
we talk.

This kind of persistence, the gentle but firm standing by, is one of the most critical things you can offer. If Stacy were able or willing to get help on her own, she would have done it by now. The fact that she hasn't, shows you she is resisting, avoiding, and denying, and needs someone like Ann, who will not turn away from the problem, but who will persist compassionately. At some point, if Stacy doesn't relent, Ann will need to move on to the next step, gathering her allies. That is the topic of the next chapter.

Leave Room for Mixed Feelings

In the 1980s, two psychologists, William Miller and Steve Rollnick, developed an innovation in counseling individuals with addictions. They called it *motivational counseling*. It means taking a non-confrontational approach to a person who is having problems and who needs to change. Their work began with addicts, but progressed to others, and was exported to a variety of settings outside traditional office-based counseling. They recognized that most people are resistant to change in varying degrees, some more than others. Some of that resistance shows up as "denial"—a person asserting that there is no problem or that the problem belongs to someone else. Miller and Rollnick developed an approach that allowed a person to express *mixed feelings*, also called *ambivalence*.

Motivational counseling is based on listening, particularly paying attention to *any* time a person actually expresses some kind of acknowledgement that he has a problem, no matter how slight the acknowledgement, even though it may be in the midst of other sentences denying that there *is* a problem. Those statements are noticed out loud by the person listening, asking for more examples. Compassion and empathy are expressed by affirming that change is indeed hard, even while noticing that the person says that he *might* be interested in doing something about the problem himself.

The assumption of this approach is that, at some level, the person you are facing *knows* that there is a problem. He may have already done what he can on his own to address it, and may be demoralized about his lack of success.

Javier: *What's going on at work this week?*

Maria: *It's really getting bad.*

Javier: *In what way?*

Maria: *I lost my temper and screamed at Henry when he didn't have the report to me on time. I said some mean things to him again.*

Javier: *Oh dear. Again?*

Maria: *For the last month I have been so irritable, especially toward Henry. I'm scared he's gone to HR to make a complaint about me, and they're building a case to fire me.*

Javier: *Sounds like you aren't happy with how you are handling Henry.*

Maria: *I'm just as upset with myself as I am with him. I've tried to not yell at him, but I can't help it. Maybe it's because when I do yell, he actually gets stuff done. I can't stand people like that!*

Javier: *Sounds like you have been trying to keep your cool and it's been hard. Kind of like me when I tried to stop smoking.*

Maria: *I'm not doing so well.*

Javier: *You sound frustrated with yourself, unhappy with your temper. I can see why it's hard. Though you're trying, you don't seem to be getting as far as you want. That must be tiring. Since you are trying as hard as you can, maybe you need something more to help.*

Maria: *Like what?*

Javier: *Like talking to somebody who knows about how people struggle with their tempers, and can give you a few tips about how to deal with yours better; maybe even help you find a different way to motivate Henry; maybe someone who can see what you've already tried and build on it; someone who understands the psychology of people like Henry.*

Let's break down this conversation:

1. Javier starts with an open-ended question. Rather than asking something that can be answered with yes or no, he asks a question that elicits a broader response. He expresses non-judgmental concern: "Oh dear!"

2. He focuses on the fact that there is a chronic and recurring emotional problem here, simply by saying "again?"

3. He affirms Maria's efforts to change by under-scoring that she is trying hard, and she herself is frustrated that she hasn't been able to change.

4. He notes that she has mixed feelings about changing, with negative feelings toward Henry and some toward herself and her own lack of control. He lets her have *both* feelings, rather than forcing this to be all about her (or all about Henry) and risking her getting defensive. It is about Henry, but it's *also* about Maria. By letting both truths co-exist, Javier is linking the truth about Maria to her already established truth about Henry.

5. Javier sympathizes with how exhausting it is to have given your best shot and not succeeded in changing the problem. He notes a number of times that he sees Maria trying, giving her some *positive* feedback. He further sympathizes with her about how hard it is to change, by comparing it to his own efforts to quit smoking (empathizing through self-disclosure, a way available to a family member or friend, but not usually to a psychiatrist).

6. He finally goes on to suggest that she might be able to benefit from additional help, not to invalidate her efforts, but to build on them. She seems to half-acknowledge that she has a problem, has worked on it, and *wants* things to be better. Javier also adds that the "expert" helper might be able to give her some tips about how to handle Henry's problems. Again, the whole story isn't about Maria's problems. Particularly note that Javier's emphasis is on the *added value* of professional help, rather than on Maria's being damaged or broken, creating a feeling of hope and help, rather than shame or humiliation.

He also takes some of the focus off Maria by implying that the professional may be useful to advise her about *Henry's* mental state. That may be a less threatening entrée to a consultation.

They Don't Have to Believe They Need Help

Remember, the goal is to get your friend to go for that initial visit. To do that, you do *not* have to tell her that she might be sick, have a big problem, be mentally ill, or need to have her "head examined," or that the problem is *hers*. The message could be simply: *You are having a difficult problem with _____ (your mood, your behavior with a coworker, your mother, controlling your drinking, etc.). You've tried hard to wrestle with it. You are worried a bit about yourself (a very key thing to notice). There may be additional ideas, strategies, or resources that can help you, offered by a professional who deals with these kinds of problems all the time.*

If a psychiatric disorder is involved, *leave it to the professional* to tell the patient after the initial assessment. That is the job of the doctor or mental health professional. Telling someone that something is the matter with her, that she is broken, abnormal, or struggling with something beyond the reach of mere willpower is the difficult job that psychiatrists and others in the field are trained to do. Often, it isn't even true that the problem is about being "sick" or "abnormal." Diagnosis is only half the skill. Conveying the diagnosis, outlining the right treatment, and recruiting the patient into that treatment process is the other half. Leave that job to the professional. Your role is not to analyze, make conclusions, venture a diagnosis, or figure out how to treat the problem. It is to just get the person you care about to show up at that office, for the first time.

Now that you have learned how to listen, to help the other feel safe, to tolerate his anger, and to let him express ambivalence, you are ready to get to the point: "You need some professional help."

Admit Your Powerlessness, Admit Your Own Need

Remember, in chapter 3, reading about the First Step in Twelve Step programs: powerlessness? Remember how paradoxically empowering it can be to actually own up to powerlessness and admit that you can't control a situation, or don't know what to do, or have tried everything you can think of without results? That is the message to communicate to the person you are trying to help: *this situation is beyond me, and we need someone who is used to sorting out these kinds of problems and can give some suggestions about how to help*. In a way, the message is that *you* need help because you are worried and concerned, but you don't have enough knowledge or experience to figure out how to help. This lets you move from the idea of you as the helper to the professional as the helper. Transferring the "need" to yourself can be a very effective strategy. This is when you can move beyond empathizing and express your worry and concern as you implore, "Please get some professional help!"

Javier: *I have really been worried about how you are feeling. In fact, I don't really know what I can do for you besides just offering you my support.*

Maria: *Well, that's enough.*

Javier: *I don't know. It's not enough for me actually. I feel like I don't know enough to help you. In fact, sometimes I worry that I might actually say or do the wrong thing.*

Maria: *Sometimes you do. You made me really mad the other night when you told me to just stop crying all the time.*

Javier: *That's what I mean. I don't want to make things worse. So, I'd like to go with you to talk with someone who has a lot of experience with people who have emotional problems, someone who can give some guidance, not just for you, but for me, too, so that I can help and not accidentally make things worse.*

It's a real contribution for you to admit your own powerlessness. It makes you less threatening because you are now in a more vulnerable posture. It also models for the other that it's okay to feel powerless. Finally, you are modeling the idea that professional help might be valuable to you in the face of that feeling so, by extension, it can be valuable for the other person. In essence, Javier is saying to Maria, "We are both not coping well, and you are not alone in feeling vulnerable." Javier is coming "down" to help Maria "up."

In the next chapter, you'll see that sometimes it is desirable to get your *own* consultation with a mental health professional, even before you approach the other of your concern, to fortify yourself with support, knowledge, and a plan. Many people approach me for just such a need—not for their own mental health problem, but to brainstorm ideas to help another. So, it's quite true that the helper can sometimes feel rather helpless; that alone is often the reason for a consultation.

The "do it for *me*" approach can be very persuasive. "Do it for the kids" or "Do it for Mom and Dad" are variations on the theme. This strategy can be enhanced by casting the request to get help in the form of a gift for one's self or another important person in the other's life.

Ask for a Gift

Sally had been concerned about her husband's irritability, explosive temper, bouts of drinking, and terrible insomnia for months. She had expressed her worries to him, sometimes triggering the very explosions she was talking about. Occasionally, Zach would apologize, but often not, which only made Sally more demoralized. After Thanksgiving, as every year, Zach (who, despite his problems, could be thoughtful at times) asked Sally, "Do you want anything special for Christmas this year?" Sally jumped at the opportunity. "I am so glad you asked. Usually, I don't know what to ask you for, and have to think really hard about what I want. This year though, it's easy. First, let me tell you what I don't want this year. I don't want something you can buy in the store, a material object, anything you can put in a box. I want one thing, something that I would consider a bigger act of love than anything you have ever given me." Zach was eager, ready, "What's that?" "I want you to agree to a one-time visit with a psychiatrist about how you are doing. I want that as a gift for *me*," requested Sally.

It worked. Later that month I met with them in my office for the first time, and they told me the story of how they got there.

Here are some other approaches I've seen work that ask for a gift:

- "Getting a consultation with a psychiatrist about your mood swings would be the best thing you could do for our little girl's birthday. It's better than anything else that you could possibly give her. Please, do it for her.

She, more than anyone, needs you to get some direction and proper help, more help than I know how to give you."

- "We've been friends for years, and we've been there for each other during good times and bad. I need you to do this for me, in honor of our relationship. I would consider it a gift to me if you were to consult a professional about this problem."

- "Your brother and I have been talking, and we're so concerned about how you have been feeling. It would mean so much for us, if you would give us the peace-of-mind to know what's going on and see you get some help. We'd like to do whatever you need to help you get evaluated by a professional who would know how to understand what you're feeling and be able to help you. Please, do this for us."

When I evaluate a patient, I typically find that the problems have been going on for a while. I always ask, "Why now?" It's not unusual to hear that patients finally decided to come in because of concern for their child or children. This is not only true of women, but men as well. The feeling of responsibility toward children can often mobilize people's actions about their own health, both physical and mental. (It is also a very common reason that people who are suicidal do not act on those feelings—because of their children.) By the same token, I have commonly heard that people came in because a spouse or friend strongly suggested it (sometimes even coerced them to come in—see chapter 8). Commonly, that person is sitting in the waiting room.

Suggest a One-time Visit

Sometimes it's preferable to suggest a single consultation rather than painting a challenging vision of "treatment." Psychiatric treatment naturally (and sometimes appropriately) conjures up a long-term commitment to repeated and frequent sessions spanning weeks, months, or even years, and fear of a lengthy involvement is one of the reasons (discussed in chapter 3) that people avoid seeking treatment. It is true that, compared to most other medical encounters, psychiatric treatment tends to be a more time-consuming and bigger project. In fact, even compared to a chronic disease like diabetes, psychiatric treatment is more time intensive, requiring thirty- to sixty-minute appointments, often a few times a month. These are not the fifteen-minute visits with a primary care physician every so often that a condition like diabetes might require. For a reluctant person, it can be too daunting to envision treatment. Getting the person to commit to treatment is the job of the psychiatrist who does the initial consultation.

I did not learn to ski until I was an adult, so I was naturally scared. I remember my ski instructor standing with me at the top of the hill, saying, "Don't look all the way down the hill; it will freak you out. Pick a tree on your right, and ski slowly toward it. When you get near it, pick out a tree on the opposite side of the slope and ski toward it. Keep repeating this process and, before you know it, you'll be at the bottom of the slope." Using this same psychology, urge the other to simply visualize a single consultation, a sit-down with an expert to present the situation and see what that expert has to say. Trust the professional to take it from there. In fact, you don't even know if there is a *bona fide* problem. It's the professional's job to lay out a vision of the way forward and persuade the patient to "ski to the next tree."

One of the things psychiatrists learn to do in training is to set people at ease and garner their interest in moving forward with solutions to their problems. This is, frankly, the expertise you need; not just expertise in diagnosis and treatment, but also in how to create a *treatment alliance* with a new patient. That is a special skill in its own right, and not one that you have to learn or try to deploy. You just have to get the other into that office.

Share Your Own Beneficial Experience with Treatment

It is a common feeling for people who are being told they might need to see a mental health professional to feel like they are being called weird, unusual, or different. This is part of the stigma, discussed in chapter 3, which causes so much reluctance to seek treatment. Consider Shirley's story.

• SHIRLEY •

Shirley's son Don was concerned when she became increasingly irritable. At eighty-two, her memory was sharp, but she had started to become less patient with people, and more apt to see them as threats and obstacles to having her needs met. She would lose her temper and scream at people, even in public. Shirley had embarrassed Don when she yelled at a cashier she thought had short-changed her (the cashier had not). One day, a woman took a parking space Shirley wanted. Shirley got out of her car and threatened the woman with her cane. The woman pressed charges for assault. Don was able to get them dropped, but now he really wanted his mother to get a psychiatric evaluation.

Don decided to approach the subject by telling her about his own psychiatric treatment for depression, something he had never shared before. He spoke about how reluctant he was to go at first, how he got over that reluctance, the trusting relationship he had developed with his psychiatrist, and how valuable that relationship was to him. He also shared that he took antidepressant medication "and it made a world of difference." At the end, he expressed his concern about her irritability, which had gotten to the point of legal trouble. He wanted Shirley to talk with his psychiatrist and try to understand why she was losing her temper so easily. "I think the doctor can help you handle situations without 'losing it.'" Shirley eventually agreed.

If you or someone the troubled person knows has had mental health therapy (and who has given you permission to reveal it), sharing that information can be very empowering. Consider speaking about your own experience, maybe even your own initial reluctance to seek treatment at all. Explain how you were able to get through that yourself, what happened when you finally showed up, what the process of your first evaluation was like, and what unfolded subsequent to that first appointment. (If this applies to you, the likelihood is that it went well for you and was helpful, or you wouldn't be trying to assist another person to go through the same process.) Use that experience to leverage your goal.

The value of shared experience is the core of support groups. It is arguably *the* "medically active ingredient" in Twelve Step programs. It is not unusual for people to be brought to their first meeting of AA or NA by a friend already in the program, someone who has already struggled with the initial stages of treatment and recovery. Indeed, the very structure of Twelve Step programs includes helping others get help. In fact, it is the crowning Step, the last or Twelfth Step. Though not strictly required, professional alcohol and drug counselors are commonly former alcoholics and addicts who have been through treatment and recovery and are quite open about that with their clients. My patients who have been through drug or alcohol treatment tell me that they *prefer* counselors who have "been there" and are open about it. They can speak more frankly and from personal experience. They carry the authority of experience for their patients.

The Shamanistic Model

The model of someone who has had a problem and later becomes a healer—and who uses that experience as part of his or her healing method—is called the *shamanistic* model. It comes from anthropological observations of primitive cultures where the "medicine man" gets that role after having been profoundly ill, so ill that his life was almost certainly going to end, yet he survived and healed. That experience gives him a special power and respect, and even inspires awe among the tribe who invest him with the authority to use his survival secrets to minister to other sick people. Modern alcohol and drug counselors are squarely in that ancient mode of healers. This is less true of psychiatrists or other mental health professionals. Though many have indeed had their own psychiatric problems (we are not immune from them, any more than an oncologist is immune from cancer), conventional mental health professionals have by and large not cultivated the shamanistic method. There are a few, though, who have, and they will be self-revealing if the time is right. Two particularly famous mental health professionals, Kay Jamison and Marsha Linehan, have spoken openly and even written about their own mental illness.

Former First Lady Rosalynn Carter told me the following story:

• ED •

Ed was a teenager who had severe problems with anxiety and depression, and it was taking a toll on his schoolwork. His mother, a single parent, also thought he might be using drugs to calm himself down. Despite everything his mother tried, he refused to go to an appointment with a mental health professional. She attended a family support meeting at the National Alliance on Mental Illness (NAMI) where she met another woman whose son had the same kind of problems and had gotten very effective treatment for him. So, they schemed to introduce the boys to each other, with the hope that the other boy, Sal, would eventually tell Ed about his own problems and treatment. Sal and his mom were invited over, the boys bonded over a video game, and a friendship grew. Three months later, Ed approached his mother on his own to ask about seeing someone for his problems. Later, Ed revealed it was because Sal had talked about his own problems and the value of his own treatment, that he was willing to try it.

Make the Appointment and Go Along

Research in behavioral change has shown that removing as many obstacles as possible is key to getting a person to make a change or try something new. For example, allowing employees to make contributions to a 401(k) through auto-matic withdrawals from their paychecks (but allowing people to opt-out at any time) vastly increases people's retirement savings. So make it as easy as possible for the other: offer to make the appointment for her and drive her when the time comes. Offer to wait nearby (in the waiting room), or even be available should the doctor wish to talk to you. You can leave that decision up to her, but making the offer is a gesture of great support. Sometimes it is even better to have selected a doctor in advance, and be able to explain that you have a good reference for a doctor about whom you already know something, and you are ready to call for an appointment. Indeed, you can even go so far as to have an appointment standing by so that the doctor has to be turned down by the other, similar to the 401(k) example.

> **Javier:** *So, will you help me to help you and let us use a doctor who knows how to help with stuff like this?*
>
> **Maria:** *Maybe. I suppose.*
>
> **Javier:** *Well, frankly, I was so concerned about you that I spoke with my doctor and got the name of a person she really respects, a Dr. Smith.*
>
> **Maria:** *You did?*
>
> **Javier:** *Yes, in fact I took the liberty of calling Dr. Smith's office, and the secretary said that there is an opening on Thursday at 2:00. They are holding it open. Can I go with you?*
>
> **Maria:** *Wow, I guess you're serious.*

Notice that Javier does not ask, "Will you keep that appointment on Thursday at 2:00?" He just assumes the answer is yes and skips right to, "Can I go with you?" speaking as if it's already a plan.

• • •

The approaches in this chapter will be most successful in situations like Maria's where the person is someone who is essentially rational and able to use some logic, has a trusting connection with you, and has at least a small ability to introspect. If the person you are trying to help doesn't have at least some of those abilities, you'll need a different approach. Your influence and support alone may not be enough. You might need help from important allies.

7

How to Gather Your Allies

"He that struggles with us strengthens
our nerves, and sharpens our skill."
— EDMUND BURKE

When you take on a challenge, it's good to know who your friends are, and who can help. Ask yourself: Who else is interested in this person? Who else has noticed the problem? Are you confiding in another friend or family member about this situation and your intention of approaching the person in need?

There may be someone who has a closer relationship than you do or whose feedback the person might more easily receive. There may be someone who has a particularly easy and agreeable rapport with the sufferer—a coach, a minister, a teacher, a best friend since childhood, a sibling, a favorite aunt or grandparent, or the family doctor. This ally might accompany you in your approach, or even be better suited to make the first approach, if willing.

Consider Approaching the
Family Physician or Primary Care Provider

One of the most reliable and trusted allies can be the primary care provider (PCP). A family doctor, nurse practitioner, or physician's assistant should all be considered as potential allies. The average person is much more likely to have an established relationship with a PCP than with a psychiatrist or any kind of mental health professional. Leveraging this pre-existing medical relationship can be a highly effective shortcut in the process of getting someone help, as in Sheila's case.

• SHEILA •

Sheila's mother had consulted with me regarding her forty-year-old daughter's behavior. She was concerned: Sheila had stopped going out with friends and frequently called in sick to work. At the same time, her mother had noticed a growing number of liquor bottles in the recycling bin in front of Sheila's house. She had also learned that Sheila was staying up late into the night, glued to the Internet, "doing who-knows-what," and this was cutting into her sleep to such a degree that she had trouble getting up in the morning.

Sheila was prickly and argumentative whenever her mother voiced worry about the changes she was noticing in Sheila's mood and attitude toward work, and the pessimism she was developing about her inability to find a life partner. A few times, her mother's concern had set off a rage. Sheila would be verbally abusive, particularly when her mother suggested she could use some kind of mental health evaluation. Sheila even rejected the idea of bringing up her feelings with

Dr. Wyckert, her primary care physician for nearly twenty years.

At my suggestion, Sheila's mother called Dr. Wyckert and asked if she could share some concerns about her daughter. Dr. Wyckert responded positively, explaining that she could tell him anything she wished, but that he wasn't allowed to tell her anything about Sheila (without Sheila's permission), because of patient confidentiality. Sheila's mother detailed her observations and concerns.

As a result, at Sheila's next routine appointment, Dr. Wyckert spent time asking about her thoughts, feelings, and behaviors. At the end of the discussion, Dr. Wyckert explained his concern that she might have a form of depression. He went on to describe how depression worked, what made it worse (things like drinking), and what made it better (things like talk therapy, maybe even medication), and asked Sheila if she would have a one-time consultation with his psychiatrist colleague on the first floor, "Just to see what she thinks we should do." Sheila was a little reluctant. Dr. Wyckert asked, "We've worked together for a long time, Sheila. Would you trust me that this consultation might help?" Sheila agreed and kept the appointment the following week.

Just What the Doctor Ordered

Think of how often people take advice from their doctors that they have repeatedly rejected from their loved ones. There is something about the neutrality and authority of one's personal physician that can mobilize change and healthy behaviors. (I can't count the number of times I have sat with a couple only to hear one or the other say, "That's exactly what *I've* been trying to tell you!") If the person you are trying to help has a trusting relationship with a physician, nurse practitioner, or physician's assistant, it may be time to call that professional.

You might be surprised to know that PCPs see far more psychiatric problems in the course of a year than a psychiatrist does! Besides the fact that a PCP sees more people in a week than a psychiatrist can (a PCP can see as many as three to five patients per hour, depending on the practice, while a psychiatrist can see one or two), researchers know that one in four patients in any primary care office have a psychiatric problem. In fact, a PCP can and does treat *most* of these problems without referring to a specialist because the number of PCPs is far greater than the number of psychiatrists, psychologists, or social workers. Also, these days, the economic arrangements of managed care inhibit referral to specialists unless absolutely necessary. It's more economical for PCPs to treat mental disorders themselves, if possible. And, in some instances, you may find that the PCP can provide all the help that is needed.

Primary Care Providers Can Treat Many Common Psychiatric Problems

For treating simple problems, like mild depression or anxiety, a PCP may indeed be sufficient; studies have shown that PCPs can make a significant difference. Medications for mild depression, stress, or anxiety have become much easier to use than in the past. These drugs do not always require a specialist like a psychiatrist to manage them. That is why PCPs can often handle simple and straightforward emotional disorders without needing to refer to a psychiatrist unless the case looks complicated or isn't responding to simple treatments. Because of the limited time they spend with patients, the approach of most PCPs to mental disorders is, primarily, to prescribe medication. But not always. Sometimes a short discussion is all that is needed, though occasionally a PCP enjoys doing longer counseling sessions. Short sessions may be all that is necessary, however. One study showed that a brief conversation with a PCP could significantly impact alcohol use, especially in men, reducing their drinking by as much as 70 percent! These men needed only one to four discussions (five to fifteen minutes each) with their PCP about drinking. The reduction in drinking persisted for at least a year after the meetings.[36]

Though some folks dislike consulting *any* doctor, for many, the prospect of seeing a PCP about a problem is much less intimidating than seeing a psychiatrist or another kind of mental health professional. Very often, the patient's relationship with the PCP has been going on for some time. There is a level of trust, neutrality, and comfort in being candid with one's physician, often greater than with a family member or friend.

As discussed in chapter 3, mental disorders can have associated physical symptoms. Physical symptoms can make it easier to get the doctor on board as an ally. People are more likely to make an appointment with their health care provider to check out a physical problem than a mental one.

It would be helpful for you to alert the PCP to mental or emotional issues *in advance* of the visit. If you can, go along and be present during the visit. People have a way of withholding or hiding emotional symptoms in a busy physician's office, and doctors can sometimes fail to ask about them. Studies have confirmed that questions about emotions and mental state are often not asked by a multi-tasking PCP during a regular office visit. I have found that, if alerted in advance by an interested party, a primary care physician can and *will* take the extra time to hone in on these areas.

Like Sheila's mother, consider contacting the troubled person's primary care provider *yourself*, either in person, by telephone, or even in writing. After being put "on notice" by a family member or friend that a patient may have a mental or behavioral problem, a PCP may not only want to respond but also feel compelled to. You might consider writing a note to the PCP about the person of concern and also asking for the note to be entered into the medical record. That way there is documentation in the patient's chart that an alert was sounded to the physician. Such written documentation creates a paper trail, which can be more effective than a simple phone conversation in ensuring follow-up by the physician.

You might be asked to set an appointment for your loved one. In urgent situations, I have seen doctors "summon" the patient for an appointment after being alerted by a concerned party—the scheduler or doctor's nurse calls and finesses the patient into coming in. (In some ways, the scheduler can be a secret weapon in a medical practice.)

If the PCP does not treat patients for mental problems, he or she can be effective in getting a patient to agree to a consultation with a psychiatric specialist, as in Sheila's case. The physician might make it clear that he will stay involved, that he will expect a report, and that he will keep in touch if there is to be more than one visit. This gives the patient the idea that the psychiatrist, therapist, or social worker is an extension of the personal doctor and part of the health care team. Most primary care physicians have a good work-ing relationship with at least one psychiatrist or other kind of therapist with whom they interact and consult regularly, just as they have a collegial relationship with a surgeon or cardiologist. Indeed, like other specialists, most psychiatrists build their practices through relationships with primary care physicians.

There are instances when someone would like to speak to the loved one's doctor but does not want the troubled person to know about that conversation. There is some ethical disagreement among health care providers and professional bodies about whether conversations with concerned others must be shared with the patient. If you do *not* want a doctor to inform the patient, you should make that clear up front. Doctors have different approaches to this issue, so you'll want to know their policy. Then you can decide whether you want to proceed with your disclosure. One letter written to me about a patient by a concerned other started in the following way: "I do not wish for you to share the information below with Seth. If you feel that, ethically, you must share the contents of this letter, please stop reading now, and destroy this document." That worked for me. I felt, in that case, I had to share the letter with Seth, so I destroyed it without reading further.

Involve a Close Sibling or Dear Friend

The doctor–patient relationship is a vertical one in which the doctor has more authority, knowledge, and standing than the patient. In this sense, it is similar to a parent–child relationship. This has both advantages and disadvantages. Another way to approach the troubled person is "horizontally" through a close peer. This can be a brother or sister, cousin, or friend with whom the person has a good peer relationship.

Over the years, I have had a number of consultations initiated by a sibling. It is not unusual for that sibling to have gotten some kind of psychiatric treatment herself. When the sibling has had great benefit from psychiatric treatment, she may recognize the possibility of a genetic component to her condition, see similar symptoms in a sibling, and reach out to share the positive benefits of her treatment. Sometimes, seeing a sibling benefit from treatment can inspire a person to seek treatment for himself. I can't count how many calls I have gotten from people saying: "Prozac [Zoloft, Lexapro, Cymbalta, etc.] has changed my sister's life and I thought I might be having similar problems." Perhaps the most common example of this scenario is when a parent sees the profound change that a child with attention deficit disorder experiences with a medication. That parent (often correctly) identifies himself as having had similar problems in childhood persisting into adulthood, and brings himself in for an evaluation.

Even without a treatment history, a sibling can sometimes be the least controversial figure in a person's life. This is someone who might have reflected on the quality of life or the world of feelings with the troubled person many times in the past. He or she may often be in the best position to broach the current emotional or behavioral problems, point to symptoms, and urge an evaluation without judgment or criticism and without causing shame. Not every person has such a sibling, but for those who do, this can be a vital and effective resource in the support system of allies. Siblings can follow up, make sure the appointment was kept, and check on progress. Often, the sibling gives information to the professional that is vital for the most effective treatment.

How can you find out if the person about whom you are

concerned has such a relationship with a sibling? Questions you might ask the brother or sister of your friend include the following:

- Have you seen a psychiatrist or therapist before? Has it helped you?

- Have you ever shared something very personal with your sibling and benefited from that sharing? Does he or she know how much it helped you?

- Has your relationship moved beyond childhood and taken on some adult qualities such as good communication, trust, sharing sensitivities, and honest or straight talk?

- Have the two of you had an alliance in the past, to help protect each other from stress or the misbehaviors of others, such as disturbed parents?

- Have you helped one another during previous illnesses?

Affirmative answers to some of these questions suggest that you may have found an ally. This trusted person could help promote the suggestion for evaluation and consultation, allowing you to continue to be perceived as a caring friend.

When you speak with the sibling, ask that the conversation be kept confidential, at least at first, as you brainstorm together on how to approach the troubled sibling. Unlike a doctor, the sibling doesn't have to wrestle with professional ethical guidelines about confidentiality in this situation. In fact, you may want to bring a copy of this book with you to share with the sibling ally.

All that has been said about approaching the troubled person's siblings can equally apply to approaching a close friend, especially one who has known the person for a very long time.

Clergy

Using a member of the clergy as an ally in your approach can be a powerful tool, if such a clergyperson is involved in the life of your troubled other. In some communities or subcultures, this is more common than in others. Most well-educated clergy have had some basic training in mental health issues in seminary, and often considerable on-the-job experience with these kinds of issues in their pastoral duties. Their authority is often perceived as more benign than that of a doctor, and their motives less suspected as self-serving than those of a family member or friend.

A clergyperson may be aware of a wider network of friends and connections that the troubled person might have within the religious community—others in the congregation who might also make sense as potential allies in your quest to discuss concerns and to get a professional evaluation to occur.

If the troubled person is spiritual, the clergyperson can find the language of spirituality and religion in which to embed the recommendation for professional help, making it feel more desirable as part of a larger spiritual picture. For some people, the professional approach might seem contradictory to spirituality or to be "cheating" on a spiritual discipline. A clergyperson might be able to convince the troubled person that this is not the case.

Many clergy are specifically trained in pastoral counseling or, if not, can facilitate a referral to a pastoral counselor in that particular spiritual tradition. Many clergy have well-developed relationships with a variety of mental health professionals to whom they can refer congregants when more help is needed than just talking with a pastor, minister, priest, or rabbi. Actually, certified pastoral counselors *are* trained mental health professionals. They are able to make assessments, create treatment plans, and skillfully make referrals to additional professionals, like a psychiatrist, if necessary. So, if you can get your troubled person into pastoral counseling with the help of his or her clergyperson, then—mission accomplished!

Try a Support Group for Families and Friends—FIRST

The tradition of self-help groups, whose purpose is to support both the individual suffering from emotional and mental disorders as well as his or her family and friends, goes back to Clifford Beers, in 1908. His book, *A Mind That Found Itself*, was the first published personal story of a journey through mental illness to recovery. It is beautifully written and is considered a classic. All these years later, it remains one of the clearest narratives of the internal experience of mental illness. It also portrayed some of the reprehensible conditions in mental hospitals at that time. Beers and his book had a very powerful effect when it was published, and it inspired Henry Phipps, an early twentieth century philanthropist, to give a large donation to the Johns Hopkins Hospital in Baltimore to build a state-of-the-art, humane, psychiatric hospital and academic department, which in turn allowed Hopkins to recruit one of the most illustrious psychiatrists of the time to head it, Dr. Adolf Meyer. That department has since evolved into one of the premier training and treatment centers for psychiatry in the world.

In addition, Beers's book sparked the creation of the first self-help organization for psychiatric patients and their families and friends: The National Committee for Mental Hygiene, since renamed the National Mental Health Association and now known as Mental Health America. It is alive and well today, with over 330 affiliates nationwide (to learn more call 703-684-7722 or visit www.nmha.org). Its mission is "promoting mental health, preventing mental and substance use conditions and achieving victory over mental illnesses and addictions through advocacy, education, research and service." The organization can provide you with educational materials, advice, lists of professionals in the area, and much more.

From these roots, other self-help organizations have developed, like AA (Alcoholics Anonymous), and support groups for other diseases have flourished, too. Another superb organization that supports the family and friends of the mentally ill is the National Alliance on Mental Illness (NAMI). Local chapters meet regularly in most communities across the United States to discuss challenges, ideas, innovations, and political advocacy. An excellent way to prepare yourself to approach your psychiatrically ill loved one or friend is to attend a meeting (or two) of your local chapter of NAMI (703-524-7600, www.nami.org). This access to a nationwide group of families (over 210,000 in 2011) who have mentally ill members will provide you with tremendous support. These people have been where you are now—faced with someone who has signs of a mental disorder, who may not see the problem himself, and who had to be convinced to take that first step to get psychiatric treatment. They are a rich repository of experience as well as creative ideas, which they are very willing to share. The value of such a support group is important, not only for the ideas that can be gleaned but also for the understanding, caring, and familiarity that can be enjoyed.

Many NAMI chapters have implemented a twelve-session curriculum called the "Family-to-Family Education Program," a specialized format in which experienced families pass on wisdom to a family just beginning to deal with a mentally ill loved one or friend. Do not underestimate the value of attending such a support group, or series of classes, *before* you approach your friend or loved one. Recognize and embrace the wisdom of veterans!

Find More Allies in Books and Media

Since Clifford Beers's book in 1908, there has been a stream, if not a river, of memoirs written by individuals who have suffered from any one of a variety of mental disorders. It is not surprising that most of these books were written by people who *recovered*. Recovery provides a good reason to write. It is not unusual for me to give my own patients memoirs related to their condition to read on their own. Similarly, when consulting with people who want my advice about approaching a disturbed family member or friend, I will recommend a relevant memoir. They get a great deal from these books and view the authors as natural allies. Such books often contain descriptions of symptoms that are familiar to my patients and make them feel less different and strange. Typically, those who write such memoirs have had a severe illness (making for a good read); by comparison, the reader finds that his typically less dramatic illness can be viewed from a better perspective. He learns that treatment can be successful for a case more difficult than his. And sometimes, memoirs contain scientific and medical information on the disease and the state-of-the-art treatment options. That is very encouraging to the patient and family. Incidentally, I often ask my patients to pass on the memoir to a family member, such as a spouse, since it can give a more eloquent insight into the experience of the illness than the patient often can articulate.

The problem, though, is that such memoirs are most enlightening for those facing the diagnosis of the writer—whether that be bipolar disorder, or schizophrenia, or obsessive-compulsive disorder. Gaining insight from a memoir *before* a psychiatric consultation means you believe you already know what the disorder might be. This could lead to some inaccurate conclusions and assumptions.

At the beginning, I promised that this book would not require you to know the diagnosis in order to achieve your goal of persuading the other to get help. When a family or friend consults me about someone of concern, I can usually pick up enough information to make a reasonable suggestion about a book to read. My hope is that readers will be able to discern the similarities to or differences from the problem at hand and know themselves whether the book is on track for them. If you are choosing a book on your own, you'll have to make your best guess. Frankly, it's not always hard to know the right ballpark: addiction, mood problems, psychotic symptoms, anxiety, etc., are conditions that present themselves pretty clearly.

On a few occasions, I have recommended that a particular memoir or self-help book be given to a troubled person who has not yet been evaluated. Such books can sometimes "hit the spot" and tip a person to get help. I have seen this approach lead to an evaluation that would not have been considered otherwise. Indeed, people write memoirs with the hope of inspiring the reader to get help, and to give the message that treatment works. It is not unusual for phone calls to my office to increase after a TV talk show airs an interview with the author of a memoir of an illness such as obsessive-compulsive disorder, depression, or schizophrenia. I call these "Oprah referrals." Similarly, many people come to the first appointment with a book in hand, typically a memoir, though not uncommonly it's a general book about a particular condition written for the public. The most common examples are books about attention deficit disorder, depression, or borderline personality disorder. These patients are typically self-diagnosed and want to be formally evaluated. Interestingly, they are frequently right, though not always. The knowledge gained from reading an entire book is usually far deeper than, say, reading a magazine article or a few pages on the Internet. That's why people who have digested an entire book, and can identify their experience, are often diagnostically correct about their conditions. Sometimes, though, I have to convince a new patient that his self-diagnosis is inaccurate. I find that this is typically not too difficult, however, if I explain the differences clearly. Even so, I am grateful for the book to have at least brought the person through the door, even if she comes with an inaccurate conclusion.

In the resources section on pages 251–253, you will find a list of memoirs I recommend in my practice (both for current patients and prospective patients) that illuminate some common mental health problems.

Movies

There are also a number of good movies that portray psychiatric disorders in the context of a person's life. Some are based on biographies (e.g., *A Beautiful Mind*). Others are fictionalized, but well-informed nevertheless. David Robinson's book, *Reel Psychiatry: Movie Portrayals of Psychiatric Conditions* (Rapid Psychler Press, 2003), is an excellent compendium of movies illustrating common psychiatric conditions. You'll find an extensive list of my favorite movies and documentaries in the resources section on pages 253–256.

Internet

The Internet can be another good source of information and potential allies. The challenge is to separate the credible sites from the fringe. Information about mental illness in general, and links to helpful memoirs, can be found at the following highly respected websites:

American Psychiatric Association: www.psych.org

American Psychological Association: www.apa.org

National Alliance on Mental Illness: www.nami.org

National Institute of Mental Health: www.nimh.nih.gov

Not only is the Web a source of general and specific information, it can also provide support with chat rooms, listserves, and bulletin boards for those who have emotional disorders and those who care about them. A more extensive list of credible and helpful websites can be found in the resources section on pages 241–247.

Get Your Own Psychiatric Consultation for Guidance

Besides educating yourself with books, movies, and websites, you may want to go one step further, and schedule your own appointment with a psychiatrist or other mental health professional. Over the years, I have held countless consultations with people who have come to see me not about *them-*

selves, but about someone else. In fact, about 10 percent of my practice is precisely this scenario. These individuals come to talk about the dilemma they face with someone they care about (typically a child, sibling or parent, close friend, or even a neighbor), who is having psychiatric problems. People who consult me in this way either do not know how to approach the troubled person or *have* tried to convince that person to get psychiatric help or *stay in treatment,* but without success. For some, a single meeting is enough to arm them with suggestions they can quickly implement. Occasionally, we have needed a few visits to plan a strategy or to build an intervention in stages. Sometimes this consulting relationship lasts a while, through many chapters of the others' problems. If any one particular approach to the troubled other doesn't work, we can keep meeting to pursue more ideas. This kind of consultation can also result in calling in additional interested parties or relatives to recruit a larger group of allies, which will have an even greater chance of being effective. Nick's story provides a helpful example of how this can work.

• NICK •

Nick had had a successful freshman year at Vanderbilt. Over the summer vacation that followed, however, he developed an unusual interest. Where formerly he could never get enough time on the tennis courts, he was now holed up in his bedroom, reading books about mysticism for weeks on end. His family overheard him talking to himself in his room, as if someone else were there with him. From the scent emerging from his room, it was clear he had begun smoking marijuana on a daily basis. His parents had tried talking with him about their concerns, telling him they were worried, insisting that marijuana was not allowed in the house. (He got around one concern by going to the woods behind the house to smoke, where he kept a stash of marijuana hidden in a tree trunk.)

It was now the end of summer and Nick declared that he had no intention of returning to college, because he was educating himself by reading far more important mystical texts from various traditions. His parents urged him to see a psychiatrist to "just talk about what you're feeling." He refused, telling them, "It's my decision. There is nothing wrong with me. If you guys have such a problem with me, then you should see a psychiatrist."

That is exactly what they did. They came to see me and asked how to proceed with Nick—how could they convince him to get help? We ended up meeting about six times, since we had to try a few different approaches until we finally hit on one that worked. We started with the gentlest approaches, in which I coached them about some of the facilitated communication techniques described in this book. Eventually, it took a stronger use of their power as parents, one of the more "coercive" approaches, discussed in chapter 8. In this way, I did eventually meet Nick, and we continue working together, now over a year later, with remarkable progress. He was able to return to Vanderbilt after needing a semester off for his treatment of bipolar disorder, for which he was self-medicating, using marijuana, which was starting to tip him into psychotic symptoms.

Sometimes, those who are consulting me are themselves so wounded and exhausted from dealing with an untreated mentally ill loved one that *they* need some healing themselves before they can be ready for effective intervention. This turns out to be very important. (Remember the emergency rule from chapter 1: on the airplane, you should secure your own oxygen mask before helping a child.) Part of the overall plan for helping the ill person might include support of the prospective helper. This is especially common in situations involving a mentally ill spouse or child. For example, in the case of Alzheimer's disease, where there is currently no treatment to reverse its progressive course, the most significant way a psychiatrist can be effective is to help the *caregivers,* who can be crushed under the burden of their relative's deterioration. All kinds of psychological disturbances may occur in the caregiving family. Often, I find that the helper in these situations is herself suffering from a stress disorder, clinical depression, or anxiety disorder that needs attention. The dementia in a parent may have profoundly affected a relationship with his or her children or the children's relationships with each other.

By the way, it is *not* a "given" that the mental health professional is going to point out *your* need for psychological help. The consultant shouldn't reflexively turn the tables on you. Keep in mind, though, that a series of consultations might result in an unburdening, and open you up enough to benefit from some help with your own emotions.

Sometimes my input in such consultations is helping the helpers to not make things worse. Your reactions to the troubled person can sometimes escalate the situation—pour gasoline on the fire so to speak. Then, when the fire rages hotter, it is harder than ever to approach the other with the goal of evaluation and treatment. So the primary mission is sometimes to at least keep things as calm and rational as possible. That, too, can be an incredibly valuable reason to consult a mental health professional, *prior to* making your approach to the troubled other.

In addition to direct treatment of mental problems, psychiatrists or other mental health professionals are a source of information, networking, and referral. Much of my work in such consultations provides information about other sources of support, such as the National Alliance on Mental Illness, or some local support groups for families of people with mood disorders, or Al-Anon and Narc-Anon for families of people with substance abuse problems. Mental health professionals are highly aware of agencies, benefits, programs, and a variety of resources out there to help people with psychiatric problems and their families.

Your Own Mental Health Care Provider Can Be an Ally

It's not uncommon for a psychiatrist to work with a person for a while and determine that the "patient" that really needs help is the *relationship*. If you are in treatment yourself, and the primary focus of your work has been about coping with a difficult relationship, you might be trying to convince your spouse or significant other to join you for couples counseling.

There is an effective approach you might consider. When I am working with a patient who is struggling with a troubled spouse, or in a troubled relationship, with my patient's permission I write a letter to him or her, with the understanding that the letter will be shown to the significant other. Here is one example of a letter I wrote:

Charlie, you asked me to write to you and share some thoughts about our work together so far. As you know, most of our sessions have been about how to cope in your marriage, which is very stormy. You have often expressed some distressing feelings such as helplessness, hopelessness, fear, anger, and concern for the effect that the relationship is having on the children. I, too, have had some concerns about the children's mental health and the effect that this turbulent relationship might be having on them. The original reason you came to consult me was because of depression and anxiety. Though I am doing my best to help those problems, I have come to realize that there is only so much I can do to help you with medications and our therapy sessions. Much of your depression is related to your stress, specifically related to how your marriage is going. In addition to helping you, I also think that your marriage is a "patient" that needs help, too. Unlike you, that patient really hasn't had the benefit of professional help yet. Medication and our therapy have helped, but have only brought you so far. To bring your recovery from depression to a higher level, and for the sake of your children, I strongly recommend that you consider going with Anita to an expert who can help both of you strengthen communications, build trust, develop problem-solving skills, and figure out better ways to cooperate in parenting the children together. I'd be glad to recommend some names of professionals who specialize in treating couples. This is the "prescription" that I think would make a very big difference, not just for you, but for your whole family.

This approach often works by shifting the focus from one person to the relationship. A letter from the therapist is one way to communicate to the significant other, even if he or she has not been willing to come in and talk. Also, the letter implies that the couple can work with someone else, not the existing counselor, so that the partner doesn't feel shadowed by any bias resulting from the relationship the therapist has established with the spouse. It sets up a scenario in which they can start fresh with another professional who has a balanced perspective on the dynamics of the relationship from the opening session. Consider discussing this approach with your own counselor, if appropriate. In this way, your psychiatrist or therapist can be an important ally.

* * *

At this point, you have tried to approach the troubled person with active listening, facilitated conversation, and heartfelt requests that he or she get consultation. You have gathered a number of allies and others who care about the person and convinced them to wield their influence. If you find that your mission—to get your loved one to that first consultation—still hasn't been achieved, it's time to up the ante and apply more pressure. You need more than personal persuasion can provide. You need the power of consequences and the strength of group action.

✳

8

How to Move from Persuasion to Coercion

"She said, 'The people demand solutions!'
I said, 'There are no solutions, only trade-offs.'"
— THOMAS SOWELL

You Can't Always Count on Logic

When you use logical arguments to persuade someone to see your point of view, an underlying assumption is that the listener is rational and/or intellectually open. When you are dealing with problems in mental health, there are circumstances when this assumption is incorrect. If the person who is the focus of your concern is not rational or clearheaded, your actions so far (speaking openly and lovingly, asking for what you need, and recruiting others who have influence) may have failed. Perhaps the person you are approaching has one of the many mental disorders that impairs insight and rationality, or she denies that anything is amiss, or blames outside factors for her problems.

You have pushed all the persuasion tactics within your means, yet have not been able to convince your loved one or friend to go for a psychiatric consultation. What do you do now? Your next option is some form of therapeutic coercion.

Coercion Isn't a Dirty Word

Yes, coercion. We can try to find alternative terms that are more politically correct: strong persuasion, facilitation, providing consequences, setting limits, give and take, etc. But the word "coercion" is clear and what we are talking about at this stage. Generally, coercion has negative connotations, but in psychiatry we encounter the need for it in some cases. What we are talking about is nothing more than applying pressure and providing consequences to shape a desired behavior and achieve a goal. In short, you are going to apply power to produce change. I call this "therapeutic coercion." It sounds like an oxymoron, but it captures the notion that consequential (while still respectful) and consistent means can bring about good outcomes, even life-saving ones.

The word "power" often scares people because it conjures up negative energies: manipulation, degradation, abuse. In a clinical context, however, we try to apply power in a respectful, supportive, and kind way with the intent of eventually (though sometimes only gradually) *empowering* the very person toward whom we are applying power. In fact, the application of power in order to achieve the eventual empowerment of the troubled person is precisely what is meant by "therapeutic coercion."

Coercive approaches are an area of expertise among psychiatrists, and one of the differences between the training of psychiatrists and that of other mental health professionals, as well as other physicians. Training in inpatient hospitals, exposure to involuntary commitment proceedings, participation in guardianship and competency hearings, and work with patients whose behaviors are dangerously out of control are core elements of any psychiatric residency training. This is why I suggest consulting a psychiatrist as your initial step; you may need to access the clinical skills of therapeutic coercion.

For the threat of serious consequences to be effective, one must be in a position of some kind of power over the troubled person. For this reason, this chapter is primarily for those who hold natural positions of power in relationships: family members. Other kinds of power relationships exist, such as an employer–employee relationship, but are not necessarily appropriate for these situations and might run afoul of laws (Equal Employment Opportunity Commission regulations, the Americans with Disabilities Act, union rules, etc.), which are designed to shield employees from abuses of power by employers. Also, more seriously disturbed and dysfunctional people are less likely to have jobs. Perhaps their friends have become alienated and drifted away as well. All they may have left is their families.

In over two decades of psychiatric work, I have come to appreciate that the power of the family far exceeds almost any other power in a person's life. No doctor, court, employer, or friend can match the family when it comes to the ability to influence a family member. Yet, there are few things that leave a family feeling more powerless than illness, especially mental illness. Besides feeling bewilderment and grief, the manipulative ways people with psychiatric problems sometimes behave can leave you feeling lost, helpless, even overwhelmed. If you are a family member, it is easy to lose sight of the persuasive power you have, and may not have fully used.

Coercion Can Be Done in an Ethical Way

The moral justification for the use of interpersonal power to improve a person's mental health is based on the parent–child relationship and, in medical ethics, is referred to as *paternalism,* which was discussed in the first chapter. This is an important concept in the context of therapeutic coercion. The troubles of the person you are trying to help are limiting her. As such, she is not completely "free of mind." A person with a mental disorder can have, by the very nature of the problem, diminished rational capacities. This puts a caring (and rational) person in a position to take stewardship for the other's well-being. In the case of an ill person, that stewardship is usually temporary, and implemented to restore or enhance the other's personal power (referred to as *autonomy* in medical ethics). A compassionate, healing, caretaking stewardship over a vulnerable, mentally ill person is not just ethically acceptable, I believe it is ethically *mandatory.* This approach, so similar to parenting a child and thus deeply familiar to many, can be called on in a relationship with an adult who appears to be mentally impaired.

Who decides if that person is impaired? Well, right now, *you do!* You are reading this book because you are worried and have already concluded to the best of your ability that the person about whom you are concerned appears to be less than completely rational and well. Like Nick in the previous chapter, family might be all he has to help him right now. Your goal is to get him to someone who, through treatment, can help restore healthy autonomy.

The ethical model used in psychiatry is an adjustment of paternalism to the degree of a person's autonomy. Psychiatrists treat people whose illnesses can profoundly impair their autonomy or capacity for self-care and self-determination. Gradually, the paternalistic interventions are lessened as autonomy grows during treatment. Elsewhere, I have written extensively about this from the standpoint of ethics (see my article listed on page 249 of the resources section).

Indeed, mental illness goes to the very heart of self-determination, affecting the very organ needed to make autonomous decisions—the brain. It is no surprise that this is territory with which psychiatrists are more familiar than other doctors. As such, we implement highly paternalistic interventions: involuntary hospitalization, restraints, locking an agitated and violent person in a padded quiet room, even legally administering medication, and rarely other interventions, involuntarily. These measures are all highly supervised, endlessly reviewed by regulators and peers, often presided over by legal authorities, and explored by hospital ethics committees. Nevertheless, in the treatment of severe mental disorders, they remain in place as critical methods.

Psychiatrists are only brief sojourners in their patients' lives. We spend very little time with them compared to their family, friends, and coworkers. So, it is important that I share this concept of ethical paternalism with you, the person far more involved than a psychiatrist will ever be.

The concept of compassionate paternalism can be most effectively implemented in the context of dealing with family members, especially adult children living at home. That's the scenario about which I most commonly advise people in my practice. If you are a parent, there was a time when you engaged in paternalism over your developing child. This is a path already well-trod by you and your child. As I explain to families I counsel, it is an adult's responsibility to take care of one's health by taking responsible measures to have it evaluated. In fact, it's not just a responsibility to one's self, but to one's entire family, who can suffer greatly when a member gets sick, particularly when they live together.

If an adult child who lives with you wishes to have certain privileges, she needs to fulfill the responsibility of caring for her health. It is her way of being a participating, contributing, responsible family member. If sufficiently impaired, that may be the *only* way she can participate in family life at first. If she refuses to take that responsibility, the appropriate response is to modify the privileges and benefits that flow from family membership.

Find Your Source of Power in Resources: Giving and Taking Away

When people consult with me about an apparently ill or disturbed family member, my primary mission is to *help them find their own power*. Again, the most typical situations are parents who are worried about a grown child. Usually the child is at least an adolescent, and often an adult child still living at home, or still on the family "dole" in some way. Perhaps he is being supported in college, perhaps he is getting a subsidy in some other way from the family—a car, auto insurance, help with rent. The necessities and luxuries of modern life provide a family with an array of tools to succeed in getting a troubled family member to a mental health evaluation and even keeping him in treatment.

There are two fundamental approaches to consequences: positive or negative. The former gives rewards for behaviors you'd like to see; the latter takes away privileges. Some people respond better to one approach over another. In fact, it's a common axiom in working with different personalities that extroverts are more likely to respond to positive rewards and introverts to negative consequences. The very definition of introversion is a kind of temperament in which a person is very focused on the future, motivated primarily by avoiding negative consequences. In contrast, extroverts are very present-focused and motivated by more immediate rewards. Howard's story illustrates the motivation of rewards.

• HOWARD •

Howard, an extroverted twenty-three-year-old, returned home a couple of years after finishing college to live with his parents. Highly talkative and engaging, friendly and outgoing, strongly drawn to pleasures of the moment above taking-care-of-business, he had become prone to extreme temper outbursts and incredible irritability. Twice, he put his fist through the wall in his bedroom.

Howard had not been looking for a job. Instead, he stayed up all night, playing his Nintendo DS game, and slept all day. He had done a few odd jobs around the neighborhood, but almost immediately spent his small profits on pizza, snacks, and movies. He very much wanted a Nintendo Wii system, but hadn't been able to hold on to enough money to afford it. His parents were extremely worried about Howard's behavior: his sleep habits, his lack of interest in getting a job, and his irritability, rudeness, and uncooperativeness, not to mention his wall-punching, which was so out of character and alarming.

They asked him to schedule an evaluation by a psychiatrist "just to see" what might be going on. He ignored them. Finally, they used the power of consequences and positive rewards. When he asked for a Nintendo Wii for Christmas, they explained that if he would go for the evaluation they were suggesting, not only would they purchase him a Nintendo Wii system after the appointment—before Christmas—they would get him a subscription that would allow him to rent up to three Wii games at a time. Howard liked these consequences so he made and kept an appointment within a week.

In contrast, Tyrone's parents used the tactic of withdrawing privileges, which was a more effective approach for his personality.

• TYRONE •

Tyrone was an introverted young man who kept to himself, with very few friends most of his life. Things started to go downhill for him in his first year of college. He couldn't pass his courses, spent more time by himself, and finally had to leave school and return home. Lately, his parents had heard him talking to himself in his room, sometimes even yelling to himself. His parents were concerned, and tried various conversations with him, even with the family pastor present once, urging him to get an evaluation by a psychiatric professional. He refused, and his parents eventually found their way to a consultation with me.

Tyrone's parents and I carefully crafted how they would approach him. With my counsel, they told him: "We are your parents and have an interest in your health. We are concerned about your mental health. We expect you to take responsibility for getting that health checked, since it seems to us to be a problem. We can't be sure what to call the problem, but seeing someone who can evaluate you and help our family and you is important to us. We consider doing that a responsibility as part of this family. We give you a car to drive as a privilege of being in this family. We are concerned enough about your mental health and your physical safety in the car that we are unsure that it's safe for you to be driving. So, for you to continue to have the car and for us to pay the insurance or give you gas money, we have to hear from a doctor about your mental health. We need to know whether it's safe for you to drive and, if not, what needs to be done to get you well enough to drive. We'll be glad to make the appointment if you wish, and you'll be getting the car keys back after you have that evaluation and we see what the doctor has to say about your driving safety and your mental health."

Tyrone was in my office the next week, and I diagnosed him with early onset schizophrenia (he admitted to hearing voices talking to him, and he believed the TV was talking about him and was somehow able to know what he was thinking). We agreed that, at first, we would just get together weekly. It turned out he was also smoking marijuana, which I thought could possibly be a cause of his hallucinations. He was able to stop the smoking, but unfortunately his symptoms persisted. So, a month later I convinced him to try some anti-psychotic medication. We continued talk therapy as well. A few weeks later, he told his parents they had "done the right thing."

Tyrone's parents had asserted their power over the family resources, rather than expecting him to get the consultation, merely because they insisted. It was a simple *quid pro quo*.

In a relationship with a marital partner or similar live-in significant other, there are privileges that can be mobilized as leverage for a more hardball approach if friendly, facilitating conversations (chapter 6) or bringing in other allies (chapter 7) is not effective. I have observed one woman tell her husband, for example, that she will stage a "strike" on doing laundry, preparing meals, paying for cell phones, going on vacation with him, riding in the car with him, going to social events together, visiting relatives, or even having sex with him, *until* that evaluation takes places. I have had people tell a troubled spouse they will not leave him or her alone with the children until a psychiatric evaluation takes place. These proved to be highly effective motivators.

Find Your Source of Power in Your Relationship

Implicit in the very fact that you are reading this book is that the relationship you have with the other person is precious or important to you in some way. You are using the significance of that relationship as the starting point for your approach. As you progress to more serious measures, putting that relationship on the line may be necessary. The only privilege card you may have to play is the very relationship itself. Though this is a late (maybe even final) measure, when other cards haven't worked it can be very effective.

• CATHY •

Jane and Cathy had been friends for decades (since college), when Jane became concerned about Cathy's drinking. Often, Cathy's behavior when drinking would embarrass Jane. She had expressed her concern to Cathy, suggested that Cathy consult an expert to see if there might be a problem of clinical significance, but all her suggestions were rebuffed. Jane felt she needed to set limits to help Cathy, as well as to protect her own emotional well-being. Jane told Cathy that she didn't feel safe as a passenger in Cathy's car. She explained that she no longer wanted to go out to lunch with Cathy to any restaurant that served alcohol because Cathy always ordered too much. She worried that if Cathy did have a drinking problem, Jane might be enabling her to drink more at those places. Despite these stipulations, Cathy still refused to consult a professional to determine if there really might be a drinking problem.

Finally, Jane said, "Cathy, I love you. We have been friends for years. I can't continue to watch you drink in a way that sometimes is so out of control. For us to continue our friendship, you must get an evaluation of your drinking. I'll even go with you, if you wish, and help you find the right person to see. Until we set that up, I will prayerfully put our relationship on hold. Call me when you're ready. I hope it's soon." That was an incentive that worked. Cathy and Jane showed up in my office together, and Cathy introduced Jane as "the reason I am here."

I have seen some particularly desperate spouses put their very marriage on the line, threatening to end the relationship. By that point, the ultimatum is as much for the preservation of the rational spouse's sanity as for the other person's benefit. (I hope you've picked up this book before reaching that level of desperation.) Over the years, I have seen instances where a partner temporarily moves out until an evaluation takes place. I have fully endorsed these extreme maneuvers when lesser coercions fail, especially if the mental health of the helper is at stake. In some dangerous situations, the safety of children was at stake. I have supported a parent removing himself or herself and the children from the home until an evaluation takes place, or an estranged parent refusing to return a shared-custody child to the troubled parent's home until she is professionally evaluated. I have seen adult children refuse to visit a mentally troubled parent, or take their grandchildren to visit, unless an evaluation takes place. Sometimes these situations lead to a legal response, so it's important to approach this step with proper legal counsel beforehand.

The Privilege of Residence

In the case of a troubled adult child who is still living at home, an ultimate coercive approach would be to ask that child to leave (and stay with friends, relatives, or the Salvation Army). I have seen some dramatic reversals in refusal to get psychiatric help after a few days away from the family home, or even after a night or two on the street. Many in the addictions recovery community are especially familiar with this degree of "tough love."

This is, of course, a radical approach, but it is not one that you should entirely dismiss. Making the "privilege" of residence for an adult child living in the home contingent on getting proper health care is using a very powerful benefit to leverage a very critical outcome. This is a step I counsel only in the most extreme circumstances, where the consequences of an untreated mental disorder are headed toward severe disability, irreversibility, or catastrophe. If you attend a support group like the ones offered at the National Alliance on Mental Illness (NAMI), you will likely get much support and guidance from at least one family in the group that has experience with this drastic consequence.

You'd be surprised at how often these measures work. Put something important on the chopping block, especially a privilege, and you'll get a reaction. This is especially true when it comes to mental health problems. The success of getting people into alcohol or drug treatment is well-known when, for example, the court threatens loss of their driver's license.

In order to conceive of this approach, you may have to reframe certain benefits that your loved one enjoys as "privileges," kind of like a driver's license, rather than "rights." Access to a car, auto insurance, provision of food, a home, spending money, subsidizing rent for an apartment, and so forth, are not that difficult to construe as privileges, rather than rights, for an adult child. Unlike in a marriage (alimony), or caring for a minor (child support), there are no laws mandating financial support of an adult child. So, even the legal system recognizes *any* support you might give your adult child as an optional privilege rather than an obligation.

Your Relationship Is Already Very Strained

What about the probable emotional reaction to being "threatened" by an attempt to link privileges to your specific expectation of the other? By the time you reach this point, you probably feel that the other's behavior is already putting the relationship at risk and causing significant emotional damage. Indeed, the unhappy prospect of losing the relationship may be counterbalanced by a feeling of *relief* at getting a break from it. It may be a win–win situation—a respite for you *and* help for the other. This is an important point: your self-care and preservation are not irrelevant considerations. That can be the reason you put the relationship with the troubled other on the line.

It's Not Abandonment

Some feel that holding out the relationship and its privileges for "ransom" in order to convince someone to take a step toward psychiatric evaluation is a threat of abandonment. These are highly charged words. I have wrestled with this concern numerous times in my practice. Here's how I have come to think about it. The word *abandon* comes from the Latin *ad-bannus*, which literally means "to get under control." In fact, that's exactly what you are doing, manifesting the original sense of this word by helping the other to get control of his mental life, which is out of control. You are not fleeing responsibility. You are not deserting the other person's needs. You are simply shifting *how* you are addressing the problem, creating a canal to divert the flow in a new direction—toward professional help. You are closing one door in the hope of giving the troubled person a chance to walk through the other door—the door of evaluation. Like a mother who doesn't pick up her fallen toddler, but stays away so that the child can learn to walk, you are "going away" in the hope of the other's picking himself up and agreeing to walk *where* you want him to. You'll meet him there.

When Is This Not the Right Approach?

There is an important caveat to all this. This approach is not right for everyone. If the person is so impaired that her ability to survive will be threatened, this *isn't* the right move. If the troubled person is in serious danger of harming herself or others, or can't take care of basic needs like feeding and clothing herself (e.g., someone with Alzheimer's disease), or is so irritating or annoying that others would be provoked to harm her, you need to proceed with another tactic, as outlined in the next chapter. Of course, it would not just be inadvisable, but illegal to put out or stop caring for a minor child.

One of the common concerns posed by those who consult me about a family member who staunchly refuses treatment is a fear of the danger and calamity that could befall the recipient of tough love. They worry about suicide, assault, and robbery of a sick person turned out on the streets and worse. This step is almost impossible for families who have experienced any of these tragedies. Balancing the risk of tough love against the risk to self and others when mental illness is left untreated is tricky. Even mental health professionals struggle with these decisions. They must be weighed on a case-by-case basis, and this is precisely why it is a good idea to consult a psychiatrist yourself before taking action. (As discussed in chapter 4, psychiatrists are likely to have had more experience with anything that has to do with coercion and more severe consequences than other kinds of mental health professionals.)

Safety nets can be put into place and contingencies established. I do want to tell you, however, that in over two-and-a-half decades of practice, I have yet to see even one case of death or serious danger come out of tough love actions, though I certainly have heard of that happening. On the other hand, I have seen a few people made homeless by these interventions over the years. In fact, an act of tough love by a desperate family is often the back-story of a homeless mentally ill person who is not ill enough to qualify for involuntary treatment by the standards of the law (see chapter 9), and hence remains on the streets. This is just a reminder that the level of coercion that we are now addressing is somewhat risky, but should be seriously considered as an option, preferably in consultation with a professional.

There *Is* Strength in Numbers: Consider an "Intervention"

If one relationship is powerful, many relationships together are even more so. Maybe you have seen the reality TV show *Intervention*. This term has come to mean bringing together a number of concerned people to convince someone to do something in the interest of his or her health—usually to get an evaluation and treatment. An intervention uses the power of relationships in a larger way through an assembled group of caring and concerned others. Because of the emotional intensity of an intervention, I consider intervention a form of therapeutic coercion, as it is the application of group power to create healthy change. Unlike the approaches discussed so far, it's not the power of giving or taking away. It's the *power of influence* that groups can wield.

To properly deploy this power, an intervention needs careful planning. The most successful interventions are those organized by a professional "interventionist" who can also facilitate it by being present. (Information on how to find an interventionist in your area is in the resources section on page 258.) These are almost always trained and licensed mental health professionals or substance abuse counselors. I do not recommend that you ever attempt an intervention without a professional, but I include here an introduction to the steps that an interventionist typically uses to help the group prepare:

1. Identify who should show up for the intervention (typically relatives, close friends, and clergy, if appropriate).

2. Help each participant prepare what he or she is going to say to the troubled person. Generally, each person talks about what it has felt like to experience the troubled person's behaviors (outbursts, intoxication, verbal or physical aggression, talking to himself, etc.). There is much emphasis on use of words like "me" and "I felt," rather than on finger-pointing "you" words. The hope is to communicate caring, concern, and loving-kindness. The person you are trying to help will find it harder to contradict your own feelings compared to other things you might try to address. This is the part that needs to be carefully rehearsed, and the part that, without a professional present, can easily get out of control.

3. Everyone who will participate is asked to agree to a consensus plan, which is presented to the person as the hoped-for outcome of the meeting. That plan is either an office-based evaluation or, if necessary, a more significant commitment, such as enrollment in a program for the evaluation and treatment of mental disorders (e.g., a psychiatric day hospital or inpatient facility) or a substance abuse treatment program.

4. The facilitator has helped pave the way for that outcome by identifying a professional who is standing by with an appointment, or a day program that has an opening and is awaiting the outcome of the

intervention, or an inpatient facility in which a psychiatrist or related intake admissions officer has already agreed to hold a place for admission.

5. There is typically a Plan B, or fallback plan, should the troubled person refuse to go with the group's recommendation. Sometimes that alternative path has to involve some of the consequences, restrictions, or coercions discussed earlier in this chapter.

6. Afterward, it's usually advisable for the participants to have a private get-together to talk about how the intervention went.

Here is an example of an intervention.

• ISAAC •

Isaac is sixty-four years old and has run a successful family business with his wife for the last twenty-five years. Lately, though, he has been acting oddly, accusing people of stealing items from the store. Once, he even left the shop to scream at the neighboring shopkeeper, accusing him of pilfering items. Isaac's wife, Rebecca, was mortified. She had found every item that Isaac believed stolen; they were in the store, simply misplaced. When she pointed this out to him, he was relentless in insisting there was mischief going on: if it wasn't stealing, Rebecca must have been moving things "to challenge and test me." Their relationship was starting to deteriorate over Isaac's aggressive and irrational behavior. Rebecca was anxious, unable to sleep at night, and scared to go to the store.

Their two children, Jacob and Leah, knew all about this and, with Rebecca, planned a family meeting to try to help Isaac get some sort of professional evaluation. They had done some reading on interventions and felt ready to try holding one for Isaac. Here's how it went:

Jacob: *Pop, you've been saying that someone is stealing stuff from the store.*

Isaac: *Darn right, and I think it's the ice-cream guy next door who wants to put me out of business, so he can expand into our space.*

Leah: *Yes, you've explained that to us. But, you also think that Mom is deliberately hiding stuff to aggravate you.*

Isaac: *She thinks I'm crazy.*

Rebecca: *I do not, but I think that you are getting so suspicious and it's causing you to be mean to me.*

Leah: *Dad, I've seen how hurt Mom has been when you have yelled at her. She's only trying to help.*

Jacob: *When you get so angry with Mom, and the guy next door, it really upsets me. I haven't been able to sleep at night because I've been so preoccupied with how angry and stirred up you've been, and especially worried about how Mom is coping with all this.*

Rebecca: *I'm not sleeping much myself these days.*

Leah: *So, Pop, you can see how worried we all are. We love you so much. That is why we have all gotten together tonight—to help you.*

Isaac: *Help me how?*

Leah: *To try and get you the help you need.*

Isaac: *Like what, a security guard for the store?*

Jacob: *Not yet. First, we want to get you a different kind of help, the kind of help that none of us can really give you. We want to see you get help with your emotions. You can't be emotionally beating on Mom like you have. You can't be making criminal accusations of the guy next door, only to find that the thing you thought he stole was misplaced.*

Leah: *Dad, we want you to get an evaluation by someone who understands how to help people be less upset, how to avoid taking it out on others, who can figure out why your temper has gotten so bad lately.*

Isaac: *You mean get my head examined?*

Jacob: *We want you to see an expert who can figure out what, if anything, might be going on. Maybe there is something hormonal, or maybe it's your blood sugar, or some kind of chemical imbalance. Maybe they won't find anything. Then maybe a security guard would make sense.*

Leah: *We want you to do this for us, Dad. We need it as much as you do.*

Rebecca: *I agree, and I spoke with your doctor, Dr. Moses, and he agrees. In fact, he felt that this kind of problem is best evaluated by someone who, like we said, has a specialty in this area. He recommended Dr. Komrad, a psychiatric specialist who does these kinds of evaluations.*

Jacob:	*Dr. Komrad will get back to Dr. Moses to tell him what he suggests.*
Isaac:	*When?*
Leah:	*We called Dr. Komrad, and he can see you next Wednesday.*
Isaac:	*I hope it's after the store closes . . .*

As you can see, at this point, Isaac is "in," and has tacitly agreed to keep the appointment. Although this family didn't use a professional interventionist, Rebecca, Leah, and Jacob had discussed with each other in advance how they would present their points. They knew that they should talk about their feelings, and that they would ask Isaac to consider the evaluation for the sake of the family. They recognized that Leah had a more tender, emotional relationship with Isaac so they had agreed she would pitch the need to get help with his behavior toward Rebecca. They had anticipated the "Are you saying I'm crazy?" reaction, and they were prepared to deflect that by immediately referring to a number of possible medical problems—all non-threatening. It was agreed that would be Jacob's pitch, since he was a scientist and Isaac respected him for that. They portrayed the help as *practical,* not as some kind of deep psychological probing. They had already made an ally of Dr. Moses (Isaac's primary care doctor), linking in with a medical professional Isaac trusted. They had an appointment with a psychiatrist (me) pre-planned, and emphasized that I would keep the trusted Dr. Moses in the loop.

The context was caring, firm, and persistent, and the family all stayed on point. Of course, an intervention doesn't always go so smoothly, and there are far more complex situations that would require prior consultation with a mental health professional or interventionist. Many families aren't as adept in communication or cooperation as this one.

Incidentally, they had a fallback plan if Isaac refused. It was for Leah and Jacob, every time they spoke with Isaac in the coming weeks, to mention their concern and the hope that he would at least speak with Dr. Moses about all this. They planned to keep these comments brief and not clobber Isaac. But, they were prepared to *keep the request alive*. Dr. Komrad wouldn't be mentioned again—he's an unknown. The fallback position would be to build on the well-trod relationship with Dr. Moses and Isaac's love of family. Rebecca had her own Plan B: to call Dr. Moses and ask him to call Isaac if a couple of weeks of calls from the children weren't successful. Finally, she was going to try to calmly remind Isaac how much they all needed him to get a consultation (later, at home), after every time he had one of his paranoid incidents at the store. This was a family that was prepared to not give up (more on that in chapter 10). A professional interventionist couldn't have created a better outcome for this thoughtful and loving family.

A Note on Enablers

Family and social systems are complex, and they do everything they can to maintain stability. Oddly, families often give higher value to being stable and consistent than to being functional and healthy. This means that sometimes one or more members of the system inadvertently help a psychiatric or substance abuse problem *to continue*, thinking that they are helping by keeping the peace, minimizing consequences for the troubled person, and trying not to rock the boat. This is not deliberate or malicious, but usually well-intentioned, albeit ultimately misguided. This phenomenon, known clinically as "enabling," is so common that mental health professionals typically consider who might be possible "enablers" in an initial assessment. This complex group dynamic is beyond the scope of this book to explore in detail. Suffice it to say here that interventions must be explicitly aware of those most engaged in enabling, and especially fortify those particular people to participate in the process to move the troubled one toward treatment. They may not even be physically present in an actual intervention and still could undermine it from afar. Such people are especially vulnerable to jumping ship if the intervention has to resort to Plan B, since Plan B often involves some form of challenging tough love. If Plan A is refused, such enablers can reflexively give up and move to re-institute the status quo, aborting the intervention. So, they really need the group to buttress them to cooperate and support Plan B, should it be necessary.

Some helpful books for guiding families in performing interventions are listed in the resources section on pages 248–250. Hazelden Publishing has a particular interest in this topic.

Intervention? Know When and When Not to Approach in a Group

Staging an intervention is a delicate matter, because a person having psychiatric problems is already in a vulnerable, defensive, possibly paranoid or suspicious state, and may feel that people are ganging up on her, if approached by a group. Certainly, there are times when the strength of groups, which presents a more solid wall of persuasion, is vital. The "ganging up" sensation may have to be tolerated in order to make a more persuasive argument about the need for help. However, there are other instances when this would be inadvisable.

A general rule of thumb is this: It's probably best to avoid the group approach with people whose symptoms include a high degree of suspiciousness, severe shame about their symptoms, or significant blamefulness, that is, they are seen as the cause of other people's problems. People with these features will only become more defensive and withdrawn, put up higher barricades, and go deeper into denial, if confronted by a group. Examples are people who are paranoid, manic, violent, very psychosomatic, pedophilic (or other sexual perversions), or have chronic, longstanding personality problems.

Let me clarify what is meant by "personality problems." These are people who create more suffering in others than they themselves are experiencing. There is a technical term for this attitude. It is called *ego-syntonic*. In other words, they are much more comfortable with themselves than other people are with them. You are much more troubled by them than they are about themselves. They more readily blame others for their problems, rather than take responsibility for their own contributions and vulnerabilities. Such persons need to be approached by the most trusted, least controversial figure in their circle of family and friends, rather than en masse. People to whom they give psychological permission to be "over" them (e.g., clergy, coach, beloved grandparent) are the best choices for leading the campaign to get professional help on board.

On the other hand, people who tolerate, even appreciate, a concerted approach by two or a few concerned others are typically those with a high degree of *acknowledged* suffering. These people's problems are technically called *ego-dystonic*. Namely, they feel more suffering in themselves than they are generating in others. Examples are those with depression, high anxiety, post-traumatic stress disorder, grief, or memory problems. Aside from concern for their own suffering, they are open to how they affect others. Therefore, these people are more readily approachable by groups. They can be asked to seek professional help to benefit their friends or family, as much as to benefit themselves.

Substance abusers and those with alcoholism are a category of their own and it's hard to make generalizations about people with this condition—especially as their approachability is so dependent on their relative sobriety or intoxication. It's tricky. As described in chapter 5: *Never approach a discussion of treatment and evaluation* (or any other important conversation, for that matter) *when someone is intoxicated or high*. This is as true for a group approach as for an individual approach. This may seem obvious. However, you would be surprised at how often I see family groups initiate important and serious discussions, particularly about a substance abuse problem, when the troubled person is intoxicated! Perhaps it is because such distress is associated with the behaviors that come with being high or drunk that people feel compelled to say something about these behaviors at the time. The approachers themselves may also be under the influence. As noted, this is the least rational time for the substance abuser, and the time when *you* may be most vulnerable to letting anger color your approach, so your efforts are likely to be shaming, which only adds insult to injury. It goes without saying that you should not approach if *you* have been drinking or taking substances. This is not the time to take a drink in order to "fortify" your courage!

• • •

If the power of personal or group coercion is unsuccessful and if the behavior is quite severe, you may have no choice but to move to stronger measures involving other sources of power available through the wider social system. This is covered in the next chapter, "How to Play Hardball."

9

How to Play Hardball

*"As we advance, it becomes more and more difficult,
but in fighting the difficulties the inmost strength
of the heart is developed."*

— VINCENT VAN GOGH

So far, we have looked at "softball" approaches—first, active listening, caring conversations, various ways of posing requests, and using allies, and then more coercive techniques that use both positive and negative consequences, or the emotional pressure of relationships and groups. When none of those have worked, it's not time to give up, it's time to talk about stronger interventions. It is especially important at this stage to look at all of your options, including legal actions. If after reading this book you decide to follow this course, the Seven Steps list at the end of the book provides a good checklist of actions to consider.

• MYRA •

Twenty-four-year-old Myra was brought to the local emergency room after her family called the police. For many days she had been in her room, talking loudly to herself, yelling things such as, "I'll kill you if you come near me!" They had no idea to whom she was talking. Besides that, she hadn't been downstairs or eaten in days. She refused to come out of her room. The family had been leaving food and water outside the door. Sometimes she took it, most times she didn't.

Fearful for her health, and uncertain about whether they were safe, the family decided it was time to get her psychiatric help. She refused their pleas to let them take her to the doctor or the emergency room (ER). She was in her room all day, so the family felt they had no significant leverage to persuade or coerce her to come out and go get any kind of evaluation. They were also scared because she was yelling that she would kill anyone who came near her.

Her family contacted a counselor at a mental health hotline who informed them about the process to get the authorities to forcibly bring her to the hospital for evaluation. On that advice, the police were called. Myra's parents explained to them what was going on. The police felt that she met the legal criteria for them to take her involuntarily to the hospital for evaluation. They knocked on the bedroom door. Fortunately, when they announced they were the police, Myra opened the door and they were able to convince her to come with them to the hospital. She was very upset with her family for calling the police, but they apologized and told her that they had to do it because they were so worried about her.

The family followed the police to the ER where Myra was evaluated by the psychiatrist on call. The doctor also interviewed the family to learn what was happening at home. He determined that Myra needed inpatient treatment for psychotic symptoms that had caused her to stop eating and, she admitted, had her thinking that she and her family were supposed to die, since she heard voices telling her so. She refused hospitalization, but the psychiatrist determined Myra was imminently dangerous to herself, possibly even to her family, due to a mental disorder, and so met the criteria for involuntary hospitalization in that state.

A second doctor in the ER evaluated Myra and agreed. Together, they arranged for her to be admitted involuntarily to the hospital's psychiatric unit. There, Myra continued to yell loudly to herself, talk to unseen others, threaten to kill them, and barely touch food. She did, however, take the medication that was prescribed. Because of that, the treatment team offered her a chance to become a voluntary patient. She again refused and was still quite ill, and determined by her doctors to be potentially dangerous. So, as required by law, a civil commitment hearing in front of an administrative judge was convened on the fifth day she was in the hospital. The family testified at the hearing about her behavior at home. Her hospital psychiatrist testified about her behavior in the hospital. The judge, who was especially impressed with the family's testimony, decided that Myra should continue her involuntary stay in the hospital. Myra was now officially "committed" to the hospital by the court until her treatment team deemed her well enough to be discharged. Interestingly, she relaxed after that, and continued to take her medication. Her hallucinations gradually faded away, she started to eat, and the family became impressed that she was becoming her old self. At first, Myra was

*so angry that she refused to talk with her family,
but she gradually was willing to sit with them and,
later, talk with them. After three weeks in the hospital,
she told her family during a visit, "You did the right
thing by getting me here. I was so much more sick than
I realized." They were flabbergasted, but grateful. A
few days later, she was discharged to continue her
treatment in a day hospital, allowing her to go home
every afternoon.*

Your Legal Options When Evaluation Is Refused

As discussed in chapter 3, there are many reasons people
don't bring themselves for psychiatric treatment. In some
cases, such as Myra's, despite the fact that something
appears to be *seriously* wrong, the disturbed person cannot
see it. That is why our society has mechanisms in place to
override a person's refusal for treatment. These overrides
tend to be used only in the more extreme situations. They
are more likely to be required for the kinds of problems in
mental life that are better understood as "diseases" of the
brain, which was the case in Myra's situation. However, it is
not only diseases that can cause behavior to be dangerously
out of control (see chapter 1).

This is where law meets psychiatry. In the United States,
legal guarantees based on democratic philosophies allow us
to determine our behavior. The law recognizes, however, that
there are times when people are impaired, precisely in the
faculties needed to self-determine behavior. The public
debate over "whose life is it anyway?" assumes that a person
is of sound mind, able to make the profound decision to
refuse serious treatments. At this point, you are no longer
dealing with a person who is in "sound mind."

As you might imagine, the law is fairly conservative and narrow regarding when someone is not in sound mind and eligible to have the court override her right to refuse treatment. Some very specific circumstances are required by the law to help people who, like Myra, are in need of psychiatric evaluation but can only get it against their will. Implementing these mechanisms starts with the very thing you have been trying to achieve: getting a person to an evaluation by a qualified doctor (preferably, but not always, a psychiatrist). That professional is most easily accessed in an ER or, in some states, in a special clinic for this kind of evaluation. There are even a few states (e.g., Arizona) that can send a professional out into the community or to a person's home. All fifty states have some kind of legislation that allows people to be involuntarily taken by the police to an ER for the purpose of a psychiatric *evaluation*. What happens next, after that examination, includes any number of possibilities.

It is not my purpose in this book to debate the wisdom of these laws, their ethical fairness, or their implications for democracy and personal autonomy. Others have debated this at length (e.g., The Bazelon Center, www.bazelon.org). My purpose is to teach you the rules of the system as it currently exists, and to assist you in understanding it, accessing it, and using it to the maximum advantage of the person you are trying to help.

All of the laws that enable involuntary transport to an ER, or similar centers for evaluation, start with the premise that a person *might* be having some kind of mental disorder. In fact, without that premise in place, a person can refuse to be brought to an ER for medical treatment. A person who might be having a heart attack can refuse to get in an ambulance if no mental disorder is suspected by people on the scene. To forcibly take anyone to an ER, it has to be a reasonable assumption that some kind of *psychiatric* problem is present, and it is causing potentially dangerous consequences. Once you are convinced that a serious psychiatric problem is a reasonable possibility, the next step is to go to a civil authority who can mandate that the troubled person be evaluated in an ER.

In the ER, an evaluating professional usually has to grapple with three things:

- Diagnosis: Is there an active mental disorder?
- Dangerousness: Is the person dangerous to self or others, or extremely impaired?
- Imminence: Is the dangerous behavior likely to happen *soon?*

If all three criteria are met, every state allows a person to be hospitalized for treatment against his or her will. (A movement for involuntary treatment in an outpatient setting is emerging, but that is new, difficult to enforce, present in only a handful of states and, therefore, will not be addressed here.)

Narrowness: Understanding "Dangerousness"

The behavioral criteria for allowing involuntary psychiatric treatment in the United States are not broad. They are limited to some kind of "dangerousness." Typically, the laws make reference to two types of dangerousness that can trigger legal protocols for involuntary psychiatric evaluation and treatment:

1. Dangerousness to self

    and/or

2. Dangerousness to others

In Myra's story, the doctor in the ER determined that she was potentially dangerous *both* to herself and to her family. In practice, some nuances surround these ideas that may vary from state to state. (Information regarding the laws in each state can be found at the Treatment Advocacy Center's website: www.treatmentadvocacycenter .org.) For example, most states agree that suicidal intentions qualify as "dangerousness to self." The most straight-forward example is someone who speaks of wanting to end her life. Even less ambiguous is the person who describes her plan to end her life or who has already initiated an attempt to hurt herself. Sometimes it may be difficult to know if she hurt herself with the intention of dying, or just to produce pain or numbing (a superficially scratched wrist or arm, for example). It is not for you or the police to figure that out. Remember, what we are talking about here is bringing someone to an ER involuntarily for an evaluation by a trained professional who will sort out those possibilities. The point here, indeed of this whole book, is that you do not have to figure out what is really going on, or why. You just need to get the troubled person to someone who is trained to do that.

A trained professional can usually see through a patient's denial that he or she is not dangerous, and can infer dangerousness from things the person says or has done. For example, a noose hanging in his closet, a knife hidden under his pillow, a large stash of hoarded pills, an Internet browser history showing visits to sites with instructions about ending one's life, or an expression of suicidal fantasies on a Facebook posting are evidence of danger-ousness. On the other hand, not every person who is suicidal is found to be imminently dangerous by a health care professional in the ER or other settings. Sometimes, he is sent home for that reason, with a referral for follow-up in an outpatient office or clinic.

Some states have articulated a broader idea of dangerousness, and explicitly spell this out in their laws, using words such as "gravely ill or disabled." These are broader terms, and allow more leeway. In Arizona, for example, the words are vague: "persistently or acutely disabled." Connecticut now includes the term "gravely disabled" in its criteria for involuntary psychiatric evaluation and hospital commitment. These states account for the possibility that a person can be so ill, and the illness place her in such peril, that it falls under the traditional term "dangerous," even if she has not been recently behaving dangerously or threateningly. Here are some examples from my clinical experience:

- refusal to eat for days
- catatonic immobility leading to bedsores or malnutrition
- severely provocative behavior on the streets that could incite others to violence against the disturbed person
- refusal to take medication for a serious medical condition, such as a heart arrhythmia
- a diabetic eating so poorly that her blood sugar has become high and potentially life threatening, and she is refusing any kind of medical intervention for it
- a person so paranoid that he has been too fearful to take out the garbage or get the broken toilet fixed, and rotting food or sewage is all over the house, making the residence a significant hazard to health

Some states interpret "gravely ill or disabled" as referring to the inability to physically care for one's self in the areas of food, shelter, dressing, and other essential functions. Other states interpret it more liberally to mean that a person is unable to understand he is in need of psychiatric treatment. Some will even accept the evidence that a person cannot think clearly if he expresses himself in confused or garbled ways.

News stories about violent acts committed by people with untreated mental illness are often filled with "Monday morning quarterbacks" who feel that signs of dangerousness should have alerted friends and authorities to jump into action earlier. There is often a lament, however, that the person didn't seem dangerous *enough* before the tragedy, and the system for involuntary evaluation was, therefore, not mobilized. For example, before he shot Congresswoman Gabrielle Giffords in January 2011, Jared Lee Loughner's classmates and teachers were scared of him. His outbursts and his disjointed and paranoid verbalizations in class were sometimes bizarre. But, when his algebra teacher Ben McGahee voiced his concerns to school authorities, they failed to respond because Loughner hadn't taken action to hurt anyone, hadn't provoked anyone, and hadn't brought weapons to class.

The "dangerous to others" criterion is also open to interpretation. The threat has to be readily identifiable and, in the United States, is almost exclusively physical. A physical attack is a straightforward example of dangerousness. Verbally threatening to hurt or harm someone is also recognized by most authorities as qualifying for "dangerous to others." Other examples of actions that authorities are likely to accept as sufficiently dangerous are

- keeping an apartment that is a fire hazard due to volatile chemicals (paint or other flammables) near a stove with pilot lights exposed, or consistently failing to turn off the stove
- speeding and driving aggressively
- smoking in bed
- brandishing a firearm while threatening, even if it is not explicitly pointed at someone
- making verbal threats about doing harm, even if those threats are not directed toward anyone in particular, or speaking about *wishing* harm would befall other people or institutions

Remember, these are not isolated behaviors, but they keep company with other evidence (e.g., talking to one's self, paranoid ideas, extreme depression, confusion) that a psychiatric condition is present. Not *every* person holding a firearm is considered potentially dangerous, and therefore eligible to be brought to an ER by the police—just someone who is also suspected of having a mental illness. Again, at home or in the community, it is *you* who decides that a mental illness might be present, at least at this point in the process. Later, in the ER or similar center, a trained physician or psychologist will have a chance, indeed a legal obligation, to corroborate or overrule your conclusion.

Immediacy: Understanding Imminence

Besides narrowness, the other dimension of evaluation for involuntary treatment is timeliness. Most states put emphasis on how *imminent* (that's the word often used in the laws) or *immediate* the dangerousness is. Is the person threatening *now*, holding out the knife *now*, saying she wants to die *now* (rather than some time in the future), or already starting a fire in the apartment? What *kind* of imminent danger is sometimes left vague and sometimes spelled out in laws regarding involuntary treatment. Montana law, for example, spells it out a bit: "a person in imminent danger of death or bodily harm." A few states are less concerned with the immediacy of the threat. It is often around imminence that the involuntary commitment process fails. Sometimes, a person clearly seems headed toward disaster *eventually,* just not any time soon, and the ER has to let her go. Many a disappointed family has been sent home with its ill family member who failed the criteria for hospitalization since the danger lacked imminence.

Both narrowness and imminence have been of great interest to the National Alliance on Mental Illness (NAMI, www.nami.org). This grassroots organization, of mostly family members of people with serious and persistent mental illness, has pursued legislation and lobbied to keep these dangerousness criteria as broad as possible. They fear, rightfully, that people might not be able to get help until *after* a catastrophe occurs; by then, it may be too late. If a person with mental illness does behave violently, family members are the most likely people who will be hurt; hence their interest in the easiest definitions of dangerousness in this process. NAMI has also been active in starting legislation in many states to allow outpatient alternatives for involuntary treatment in certain cases, rather than only inpatient alternatives.

At this point, don't worry about the narrowness or imminence issues at all. What you want is simply to get someone to the ER for an expert evaluation if all other attempts at getting help have failed. It is the common experience of families and clinicians who have pursued this route that the interpretation of what constitutes "dangerousness" or "grave illness" and its immediacy is much looser and broader at the beginning of the process. Courts and police are typically less strict at the point where a legal order is granted to pick up a person and take him to the ER. As we will discuss, this is the first of a three-step process and is the easiest and most lenient step. In my experience, interpretation of the dangerousness criteria becomes more stringent with subsequent steps of the process.

A Note on Terminology: "Commitment"

Many people mistakenly use the word "commitment" to describe the act of involuntarily transporting someone to the ER for a psychiatric examination. That is actually not what this term means. Terms that apply to the act of involuntarily transporting are varied. In some states, it is called "petitioning" or "an emergency petition." In other states, the process is called by the name of the state law that permits it. For example, in Florida, a person is said to be "Baker Acted" after the Baker Act, the Florida law that legally permits such involuntary transport for examination by a doctor. In other states, this process is referred to with a number, which references the statute code in that state.

The word "commitment" refers to a later step in the process, described further into this chapter, when a person who has been involuntarily hospitalized after being examined in the ER appears before a judge who decides to "commit" him to continue his hospital stay. It is not until that legal ruling that a patient is said to have been "committed" to the hospital. So, unless that ruling eventually occurs, all that has transpired prior to that hearing does not constitute commitment. If released early from the ER, or later in the hospital by the judge, the patient can answer no in the future to any legal document that asks the question, "Have you ever been involuntarily committed for psychiatric treatment?"

Starting the Process

Now that you understand how the suspicion of mental illness, dangerousness, and imminence are central to involuntary treatment, let's learn how to start the process. Most states provide three possible paths to get someone involuntarily psychiatrically evaluated, typically in an ER.

The first is not particularly relevant to this book, as it involves a doctor (in a few states, an advanced practice nurse like a nurse practitioner, or psychologist) who is *already seeing* a patient, probably in an office. That professional can initiate the process based on the examination of the patient. Some states require one of these professionals to be a psychiatrist or psychologist. In others, any certified mental health professional can do it. Again, information in the resources section on page 242 will help you to learn the law in your state.

The other two methods are for people who have not been recently evaluated by such a health care professional. This is more likely to be your starting point.

The most rapid method is to call the police, as Myra's family did. Police are empowered to determine, on the spot, if people meet the criteria for dangerousness and are showing signs of mental illness and can be brought, against their will, to the ER. The police will bring them there, as gently as possible. If necessary, the police can and will use force, such as handcuffs.

A slower method is to go to the nearest courthouse.

An official who is responsible to hear about the behaviors of people in the community will decide if an order should be issued to the police to pick up the person and bring him to the ER or (in certain states) a specialized psychiatric evaluation clinic. In some states, such as Arizona, there is actually a clinician who can be dispatched to a person's home or other location to determine if involuntary evaluation by a physician is called for. If necessary, that clinician can mobilize the police to take the person to the ER.

Calling the Police

The advantage of directly calling the police is that it's fast and simple. However, the police generally have a higher threshold for initiating the involuntary hands-on transport to an ER. They very often need to see dangerousness right there in front of them, demonstrating the criterion of imminence on the spot—like direct threats, violent behaviors, or suicidal statements. If the prospective patient behaves herself, or denies these intentions, often the police will go away. The courthouse route is slower, but the magistrate involved has an opportunity to consider broader, deeper, and more complex information before deciding to issue an order. The troubled person does not have to be present, and usually is not. I suggest reserving the direct-to-police route for very acute emergencies, where the dangerousness is imminent and obvious. Though there have certainly been stories of police mishandling the mentally ill, because of poor training, this picture is changing as awareness has grown of specialized policing techniques required to deal with the mentally ill. The Bazelon Center (www.bazelon.org) reports that there are now a few hundred training programs for these situations in police departments around the United States. The

Center for Problem-Oriented Policing (www.popcenter.org) is very focused on this issue.

Put On the Worst Face and Let Others Decide

In an acute situation, it is the job of the civil authorities to determine if the criteria are met for dangerousness or if your state's law allows the concept of "gravely disabled." It is not your responsibility to figure that out for yourself. Judges, magistrates, police, or ER physicians in your state are experienced in making this determination. Let them do it. You might not agree with their decision, but they know what symptoms and behaviors will open the doors to treatment and allow the process to unfold smoothly. The ER clinicians are clinically knowledgeable and experienced in this process.

You are critical in the first step: It is up to you to call the police or to go to the local courthouse to activate this process. That means the entire system depends on how you present the situation. Plan on giving the police or the magistrate information that clearly portrays the possibility of a psychiatric problem as well as some sense that dangerousness is part of the picture. This is the time for honesty, but also the time to put the "worst face" on your presentation. Don't lie, but find the most striking examples, the most vivid anecdotes of disturbed behaviors, thoughts, and feelings that illustrate the presence of some kind of mental disorder, plus imminent dangerousness.

The Complete Process

So far, we have gone through the process up to the point where an examination takes place in the ER. Now we can look at what happens subsequently, if the patient is not sent home.

Figure 9.1 is a flow chart of the typical involuntary process from the first contact with civil authorities through hospitalization discharge, when the person is well enough to go home.

As you can see, the process includes essentially four important phases:

1. Civil authorities are mobilized to get someone to a doctor for an evaluation, typically in an ER or related center.

2. The doctor decides if the patient needs to be in the hospital or can be sent home. If hospitalization is necessary, the patient might agree to be admitted voluntarily. If not, the doctor may decide to send the patient involuntarily to the hospital. As in Myra's case, most states require *two* doctors, or a doctor and a psychologist, to determine that a patient can be involuntarily hospitalized.

3. If a person is sent to the hospital, an administrative law judge hears the case at the hospital. This is called an "involuntary commitment hearing" and is typically held within ten days after inpatient treatment has started or been attempted (in some places, like New York City, that can happen very quickly, sometimes on the day of admission). During the hearing, it is decided if hospitalization should continue (if so, this is the point where the person is formally said to be "committed") or if the patient can be released after the hearing.

4. If a formally committed patient is refusing medication deemed necessary to make her well, a panel of clinicians can be convened to determine if the medi-

cation should be administered involuntarily. Patients can usually appeal that decision.

Not all of these steps may be necessary; the patient can cooperate or improve to such a degree that the next step need not be pursued. Then the process is naturally finished and the patient can go home. Laws and due process, established by the state, secure each step. After the first step, a psychiatrist or similar clinician is involved in every other step. From the first though, every step needs your input.

Be Present at Each Step, Especially the Hearing

By all means, being present in the ER to talk to the evaluating clinicians is essential, and may make the difference between hospitalizing your loved one or releasing her home, with a referral to a psychiatrist's office. The information you provide in the ER could be critical. If a patient gets to the step of an involuntary commitment hearing, that means the treating doctors believe she remains ill, is still potentially dangerous to herself and/or others, and needs to stay in the hospital for further treatment. As noted, in many states the hearing may not occur for up to ten days after the initial hospital admission. By then, a good deal of treatment might be accomplished. The patient may be well enough to be released home, or she may have signed a voluntary consent for further hospitalization, and the doctors have accepted it as valid. So the situation has reverted to an ordinary voluntary hospitalization and there is no further legal process. Myra was offered this option, but refused, so a hearing was convened in front of an administrative law judge. She did take her medication, but she was not well enough to be discharged before the hearing took place. That

Figure 9.1

The Involuntary Process

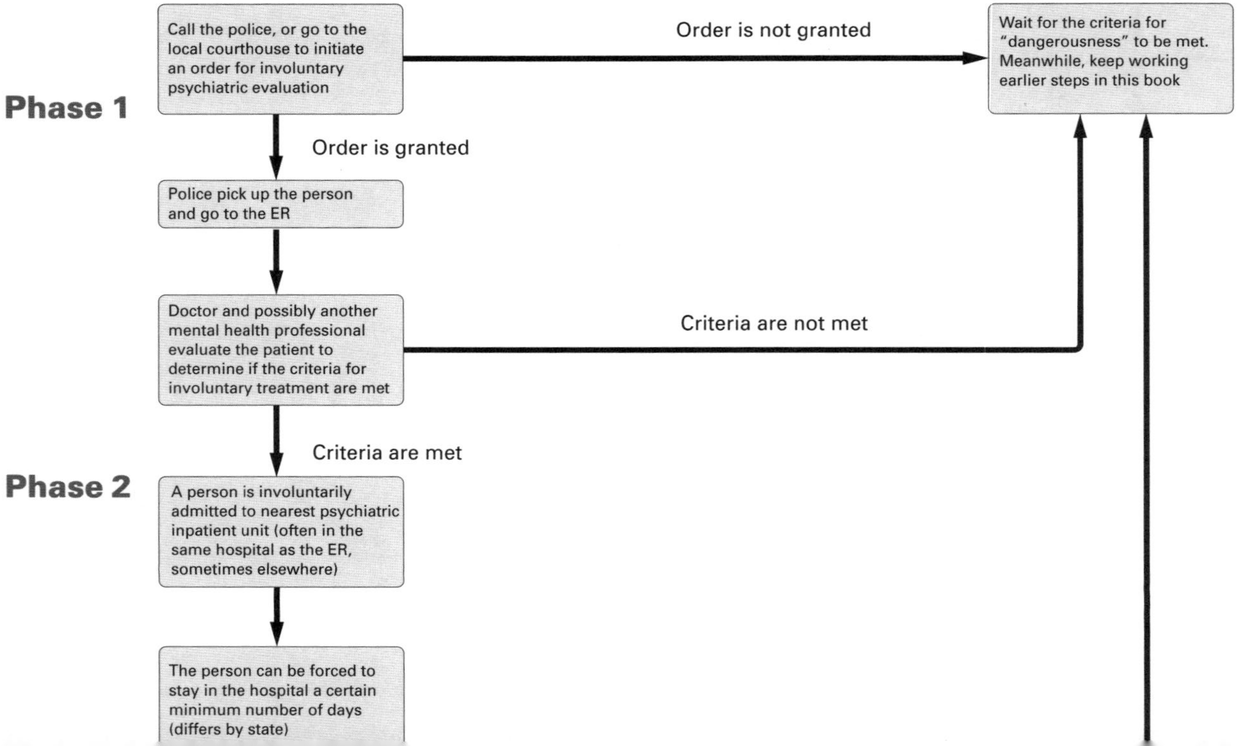

Phase 1

Call the police, or go to the local courthouse to initiate an order for involuntary psychiatric evaluation

Order is granted

Police pick up the person and go to the ER

Doctor and possibly another mental health professional evaluate the patient to determine if the criteria for involuntary treatment are met

Order is not granted

Criteria are not met

Criteria are met

Wait for the criteria for "dangerousness" to be met. Meanwhile, keep working earlier steps in this book

Phase 2

A person is involuntarily admitted to nearest psychiatric inpatient unit (often in the same hospital as the ER, sometimes elsewhere)

The person can be forced to stay in the hospital a certain minimum number of days (differs by state)

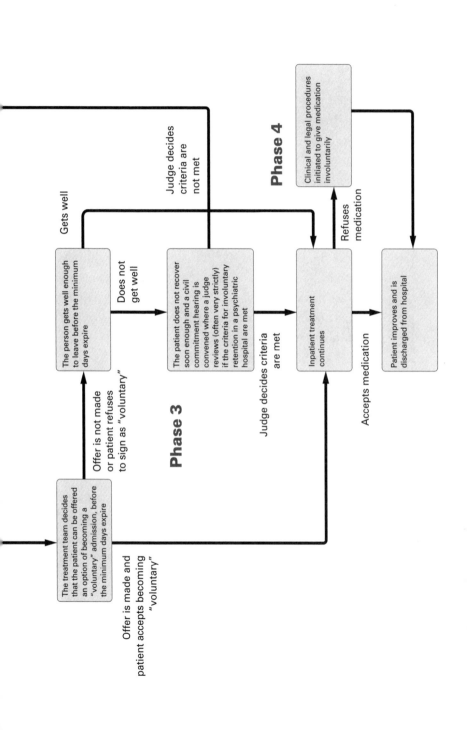

The treatment team decides that the patient can be offered an option of becoming a "voluntary" admission, before the minimum days expire

Offer is not made or patient refuses to sign as "voluntary"

Offer is made and patient accepts becoming "voluntary"

The person gets well enough to leave before the minimum days expire

Gets well

Does not get well

Phase 3

The patient does not recover soon enough and a civil commitment hearing is convened where a judge reviews (often very strictly) if the criteria for involuntary retention in a psychiatric hospital are met

Judge decides criteria are not met

Judge decides criteria are met

Inpatient treatment continues

Refuses medication

Accepts medication

Phase 4

Clinical and legal procedures initiated to give medication involuntarily

Patient improves and is discharged from hospital

was when she was formally committed to continue the hospitalization, rather than be released home.

Most patients will be represented by a public defender at this hearing; few hire their own attorney. The job of this attorney is to argue that the patient should be released, by demonstrating if and how she does *not* meet the criteria for involuntary retention in the hospital and treatment against her will. You and the doctors might disagree with that conclusion, but that is the attorney's role. Indeed, the attorney will try to find every conceivable argument that the patient should be released. This is the nature of the adversarial system. On the other side of the argument is a representative from the hospital (often not a lawyer) plus the treating doctor, who are arguing to continue the involuntary hospitalization and treatment.

If you want to help sustain the treatment process, it is vital that you be present at this hearing. You will likely be asked to testify by the representatives of the hospital in support of their effort. At the very least, you will be interviewed before the hearing. If you have important information that helps to make the case, you will likely be called as a witness by the hospital, but you will also be cross-examined by the public defender. Often more weight is given to the testimony of those who know or live with the patient than to the doctor, who may have just met the patient a few days before. If you participate, here are some important things to include in your testimony:

- Any threat of self-harm (of any sort) that you heard prior to admission, such as wanting to die or plans about how suicide would be accomplished

- Any actions of self-harm, such as cutting, burning, head banging, choking, or hanging attempts

- Any kinds of verbal or physical threats the patient made, or anything she said that made you or others feel intimidated, fearful, or in danger

- Any actions that were violent: pushing, shoving, hitting, throwing, tripping, or using any object with the intent to physically hurt herself or others

- Any actions outside the home that could have resulted in harm to self or others, such as reckless driving; walking across the street without looking; inappropriate dress for the weather that could cause heatstroke or frostbite; provocative behaviors in public that may have incited others to intimidate, assault, or threaten the patient; or grossly inappropriate and bizarre public behaviors, like nudity or public masturbation

- Any behaviors in the home that could have threatened the environment, such as leaving the stove on, overflowing the bathtub, keeping rotting food in the refrigerator, smoking in bed, falling asleep on the couch while smoking, or causing other fire hazards

- Consider bringing photos to the hearing if there is something striking about the home environment resulting from the patient's ill behaviors

- Any behaviors that resulted in neglect or danger to minors, whether active (pushing and shoving) or passive (falling asleep drunk while responsible for tending a baby)

- Any actions that could endanger an existing medical condition, such as not taking important medication for a dangerous heart arrhythmia, not taking insulin properly, or eating massive sugar meals for a diabetic

- If there are letters or e-mails expressing suicidal, homicidal, or other dangerous intentions, bring them to the hearing, or a browser history showing that the patient explored methods of suicide, information on overdosing, or how to make and acquire weapons

Be sure to make a written list to help with your recall during testimony.

Myra's family was crucial in the evaluation process at three points where the "system" needed vital information to see if she could be involuntarily treated: with the police, in the ER, and at the commitment hearing. I cannot emphasize enough the importance of being present at these kinds of junctures if you wish to maximize the likelihood that your loved one will be able to move ahead with treatment, and not have the process suddenly aborted because she is not found to meet the criteria for involuntary treatment.

Close Your Home

If the person going through a commitment hearing is living with you, and you want to help support continued hospitalization, tell the judge that she cannot be permitted to return to live with you unless the current symptoms significantly diminish. This is vital, because one of the considerations about whether it is "safe" to let a patient leave the hospital can depend on the environment to which she will be going. A person who has never lived on the streets could be in *more* danger if the family is not prepared to have her back; she will be homeless and uncared for. Or if she goes to a shelter and acts in a provocative, irrational, or peculiar way, she is likely to provoke others to violence. The safety and controls of home and family will not be available to help minimize harm to self or others. I have often seen judges take into consideration a family's testimony that they can't handle a patient. The post-discharge scenario can be critical in judges' decisions to retain patients in the hospital. "Closing your home" to the troubled person is a strategy that can work. If it doesn't, and the judge decides to release the patient, you can always change your mind (if you wish) and take her home.

If Eligible, Use the VA (Veterans Affairs) System

If your troubled person is a veteran, try to have him or her brought to a VA emergency room and admitted to a VA hospital. I have found that the criteria permitting involuntary treatment and hospitalization are looser in the military and VA hospitals, where there is a more military environment, with a culture of being "ordered" to comply, that is uncharacteristic of civilian settings. Federal law applies in VA hospitals and is sometimes firmer than state law.

Don't Be Intimidated by Fear of Damaging the Relationship

The vital importance of getting a mentally ill person to safety and returned to decent mental health needs to trump any inhibition from embarrassment or fear of alienating the troubled person or fear of damage to a relationship. It is *remarkably common* for patients to completely change their hostile attitude toward their families after they get well. That hostility is often a by-product of the illness—the distorted thinking, the supercharged emotions, and the lack of insight into being sick—all of which can be expected to improve with treatment. Myra's eventual apology, forgiveness, and validation of her family is, of course, the best possible outcome. I have seen scenes like Myra's post-psychotic appreciation of her family *numerous* times over the years.

If There Are Legal Charges, Use the Opportunity
to Require *Outpatient* Treatment

Although many people and organizations have wished for it, concerned individuals still have very little leverage to get someone into *outpatient* evaluation and treatment against his or her will. The laws for involuntary psychiatric treatment are mostly centered around *inpatient* treatment. Some states have involuntary outpatient commitment laws that mandate treatment as an outpatient, but overall, those laws are still rare and don't have real teeth; they are, as you can imagine, hard to enforce.

Fortunately, a well-established system exists for tracking people in the community and expecting them to appear in certain places, at certain times, with consequences if they do not show up: the parole and probation system. That is why it can be (ironically) fortunate, when a mentally disturbed person gets into legal trouble and has a charge pending. Here is an opportunity to get help from the legal system to *mandate* outpatient psychiatric evaluation and treatment.

• ROLAND •

Roland, a thirty-two-year-old man, was an assistant professor in a local college who had become suspicious of his colleagues, stopped going to faculty meetings, and stopped socializing with his peers. He started missing classes he was supposed to teach. His colleagues would hear him mumbling to himself. He lived alone. His neighbor, who had been friendly with him for a few years, began to hear him throwing things at the wall. His family was aware of his problems and suggested he see a doctor, even his primary care doctor, but he refused. He did, however, agree to come home to his family over spring break. Once there, he became increasingly irritable, often yelled when alone in his bedroom, and rarely left the house. Roland's parents were overwhelmed. He also started to buy alcohol. At one point, he went to the liquor store, yelled at the clerk to stop spying on him through the hidden camera in his bedroom, and threatened to call the police unless the clerk gave him some free liquor. The clerk refused, and Roland started to push him around the store. Police were called; Roland was arrested and charged with assault. His parents came to see me while they awaited a hearing on the charges.

The involvement of family or close friends is critical in this kind of situation. I advised Roland's parents that the court absolutely needed to know that there was a strong possibility he was suffering from a mental illness and had been refusing treatment for it and that the illness might well be responsible for his behavior. I suggested that they immediately contact the prosecutor's office handling the case against Roland. I also invited them to have Roland's lawyer contact me, which they did. I suggested to both the family and the lawyer that they discuss the psychiatric situation with the prosecutor and pursue a plea bargain, in which the court mandated that Roland get evaluated by a psychiatrist and participate in whatever treatment plan would be recommended. A probation officer could supervise this. If Roland violated this requirement, the court could proceed with charges and remand him to do jail time. Roland was sufficiently aware of what those consequences meant and did not want to go to jail. The lawyer and the prosecutor negotiated, and Roland was given probation-before-judgment, as long as he received psychiatric evaluation and treatment. The psychiatrist (me) was required to report to the court on Roland's attendance and compliance with treatment, which was subsequently quite good. He recovered in a couple of months and was well enough to return to his career the following semester. He continued to see his probation officer, and a year later, the charges were dropped.

I have used a similar approach for certain professionals, whose behavior has put them at risk of losing their professional licenses. Their licensing boards have required them to be in treatment to maintain their licenses or other access to work, such as hospital privileges for physicians. A very common scenario is when the state makes a person's driving privileges dependent on treatment, particularly in the setting of a DWI charge.

The lesson here is to *use* the opportunity to engage a system that has power over your troubled loved one, to steer him into the treatment he has been avoiding or refusing. In my experience, as long as the crime isn't particularly heinous (and especially when there is no prior history of criminal charges), most judges wish to be of help to the mentally ill or substance abusers, and avoid unnecessarily over-crowding the prisons. The court has to *know,* however, that it is dealing with someone who has a mental illness. Sometimes, the only way the court can know this is from family and friends. Certainly the defendant herself isn't going to make that point to her attorney or in court, often because she doesn't believe she is ill at all. The only way you can get that information to the judge is through the attorneys. Ultimately, if the opposing attorneys are on the same page, share a vision of the situation, and agree on the goals, judges will typically respond to their mutual agreement and use the court's power to enforce treatment, rather than punishment. Without the help of family or friends to broker such an agreement between the attorneys, this is a much less likely outcome.

Common legal charges where this approach has worked are DWIs, minor assaults (like Roland's), trespassing, breaking and entering, or minor drug possession. The approach is much less likely to work where a victim has been significantly injured, or if a weapon is involved.

Psychiatric Treatment in Jail

The worst possible outcome is for a mentally ill person to go to prison, an outcome all too common. It has been well documented that the penal system is where most institutionalized mentally ill people can be found.[37] Fortunately, awareness is increasing in most states (even California, where the problem is worst) that the prisons have become inappropriate alternatives to psychiatric hospitals for many of the mentally ill, and efforts are under way to turn that around, albeit slowly. The second worst outcome is simple acquittal—at that point, the opportunity to leverage treatment through the court system has been lost for the time being.

In the event that the person you are trying to help does end up going to jail, all is not lost. However, it is critical that you get in touch with the psychiatrist at that facility (there is *always* at least one doctor assigned to every facility, sometimes a psychiatrist as well). That is the person with whom you now need to communicate the history of the situation and your observations about what has been happening. Psychiatric evaluation and treatment in jail or prison is certainly not optimal, but it's far better than nothing, which is what was happening at home. You would be amazed at how much mental health treatment some facilities provide. Frederic Reamer, professor of social work at Rhode Island College, studies the treatment of psychiatric problems in prison inmates and points out, in the January 2011 issue of *Corrections Forum*: [38]

> In a typical prison system, treatment options vary depending on the inmates' clinical symptoms and diagnoses . . . depression, bipolar disorder, schizophrenia, and anxiety disorders . . . receive medication . . . Inmates who are sex offenders . . . participate in individual and group counseling . . . inmates diagnosed with addictions may participate in long-term addiction counseling . . . Some prisons provide selected inmates with individual counseling, especially those with severe trauma histories.

So, as undesirable as having a mentally ill person in prison can be, all is not lost. A few of the best psychiatrists I know in Maryland work in the correctional system. For a number of patients I've seen, jail time was a positive turning point in their lives, as it was the beginning of proper psychiatric treatment, sometimes for the first time in their lives. The same goes for substance abuse. People sometimes found their way to AA or NA for the first time while in jail and have been sober since. I have had patients for whom jail time has literally saved their lives. A couple of them still go back to the jail as volunteers to run support groups or Twelve Step meetings.

If There Isn't a Legal Problem,
Consider Initiating One

We are now at the point of the most serious of the hardball approaches, when you need to truly "make a legal case out of it." Besides involuntary commitment and plea-bargaining criminal charges, there are other ways to use the power of the legal system. There are other circumstances in which courts can mandate a psychiatric evaluation without an "imminent danger to self or others" benchmark. Getting the courts involved always heightens the adversarial atmosphere between you and the other. Creating legal battles to get someone psychiatric help is generally pursued out of the need to protect yourself or vulnerable children, rather than altruism or gracious benevolence. Although you still may care for and love the person on some level, by then the atmosphere is already in the red zone.

An attorney can help you initiate legal proceedings challenging a person's mental competency and asking the court to appoint a guardian. Under these circumstances, the court requires a psychiatric evaluation of the person in question in order to rule on whether that person is competent or not. Out of that evaluation can come an openness to treatment on the part of the troubled person, or maybe a recommendation by the evaluator for involuntary civil commitment.It at least gives the troubled person a shot at treatment by subjecting him to that critical first step— a psychiatric evaluation. The best place to start is with a lawyer who specializes in guardianship; get a referral from someone you know, or look in the Yellow Pages or the Internet. Guardianship specialization is typically listed in directories and advertising by attorneys. It is important to be aware that most states do not allow people with a guardian to be involuntarily hospitalized simply because the guardian wants it. They *still* have to fulfill the dangerousness criteria. However, certain guardianships will allow the guardian to give permission for involuntary medication or electroconvulsive therapy, *after* the patient is already committed to the hospital via the usual procedures we have been reviewing.

Another way to get the courts involved is when the welfare of a child is at stake. A parent who is highly concerned about the other parent's mental health can take this approach. In this situation, you would leave the home, bringing the child or children with you, and engage a lawyer to petition the court for an *emergency custody evaluation.* In that petition, the court can be alerted to the strong possibility of mental illness in the other parent. If the troubled person wishes to fight for custody, a court can order him or her to be evaluated. Be forewarned, this is tricky. I have seen this approach fail because the troubled parent was *too ill* to care, to fight back, or to even want the children at that point. But at least the children are out of harm's way. Moreover, if the situation is very adversarial, the troubled parent might fight back and allege that *you* are the one with psychiatric problems. In this event, a judge might order *both* parents to be evaluated. I encourage you not to worry about this. If you have your head on straight, and the other is so troubled as to bring you to this point, the evaluating professional will be able to see it.

Mental Illness and Substance Abuse Are Approached Differently by the System

Before we leave the issue of involuntary treatment, this is one place where it is crucial to separate traditional psychiatric problems from substance use disorders and other addictions.

Though clinicians regard substance abuse and other mental disorders largely in the same package, unfortunately the courts do not. The legal system treats addictions differently than other psychiatric problems, particularly when it comes to mandating involuntary treatment. Though it may be perfectly apparent that an active heroin or crack addict can be said to endanger self or others, the civil authorities see this kind of endangerment as different. First, danger is likely to be transient, only during periods of being high, or withdrawal, or the urge to use. Those intervals usually last only a few hours. The long process of involuntary treatment is generally not pursued for dangerousness that will shortly pass. In short, *imminence* disappears if you just wait a few hours. That is why intoxicated people in the ER are often left to "dry out" overnight. By the next morning, they are typically no longer a danger and can be released. Second, many clinicians might disagree, but the courts assume there is a higher degree of choice for those who drink, take drugs, gamble, shoplift, etc., compared to that of other kinds of serious mental disorders. The autonomy of addicts is assumed to be higher and, therefore, the paternalism of the state to interfere with their right to abuse substances is rarely considered necessary.

I cannot defend this distinction between addictions and other conditions; I can only educate you about it. It is very difficult to mobilize the involuntary health care assessment and treatment system described in this chapter when the problem is addiction alone. The courts generally demand treatment if an addiction is relevant to breaking the law (classically, a DWI charge). Then the court *might* mandate addictions counseling as part of sentencing or probation or give probation-before-judgment if treatment is pursued. It has become common nowadays for defendants charged with DWI to go to substance abuse treatment *prior to* appearing in court (usually on the advice of their lawyers) to help mitigate the judge's sentence when the case is heard.

By now, that first evaluation has taken place, or is about to, and with any luck, you have gotten the troubled person to the evaluation with the most facilitation and support, and the least amount of complex strategy, interventions, coercions, or legal maneuvers. However, now you know the legal lengths to which you can go, if necessary. How can you help going forward? You still have a role, you can still help.

Dangerousness and Safety

This chapter focused on situations in which danger is a major consideration. We have looked mostly at getting the troubled person to safety. Naturally, you want to keep yourself safe, too, as well as extend the safety net to others who might be harmed.

Critical in this situation is considering deadly weapons that might be available. Statistics have shown that the rates of suicide and homicide are much higher in households where there is a gun (up to ten times higher!). Most gun-related deaths are the result of suicide, and over half of all completed suicides involve guns. Suicide by gun is much more common than homicide by gun![39] So, when helping the troubled person in your life who is behaving dangerously because of a probable mental disorder (as defined in chapter 1), if you know a gun is in the house—get it out as safely as possible. Do not worry that the other might become mad about that. Trust that later, when his condition is treated, he will understand, will no longer be dangerous, and can have his legal firearm(s) back. Do not take chances, and be prepared to get police help if you cannot safely deal with a firearm situation.

Another dangerous situation calling for action is when children are at risk. Every state has some kind of agency that can protect children in dangerous situations. Now is not the time to wrestle with the imperfections and oversights in the operation of these agencies, which are famously portrayed in the media. If you feel children are at risk, and cannot remove them from the troubled person's reach, contact these authorities to help. Information about how to find such agencies in your state can be found in the resources section on page 257.

Finally, if you personally feel at risk, don't take chances. Remove yourself from the scene or, if the danger is imminent, call the police. There are specialized agencies where you can go for counseling, advice, and guidance when your troubled other is violent. The most common example is domestic violence. Shelters, counselors, and legal aid are all part of the services available through organizations that exist in every state, and most counties. The National Coalition Against Domestic Violence (www.ncadv.org/resources /StateCoalitionList.php) is an excellent clearinghouse for these resources.

10

How to Continue Your Support

"If you want to succeed, double your failure rate."
— THOMAS WATSON

Where Danger and Opportunity Meet

I have a beautiful painting in my office, created by a patient of mine and given to me as a gift of thanks. It is the Chinese symbol for "crisis."

The Chinese symbol for crisis consists of two characters. The larger symbol (on the right), written by itself, means "danger." The smaller symbol (on the left), written by itself, means something like "crucial change point." The idea is that the first thing one sees when a crisis hits, writ large, is the awful face of danger, fear, catastrophe, and uncertainty. Hidden behind that, however, is an opportunity for change, perhaps for the better—a new direction or healing.

A crisis is not merely dreadful, it's also a possible point for a change of trajectory. The Chinese symbol reflects the "yin/yang" balance between seemingly contradictory forces, which is a well-known concept in Eastern philosophies, and which the great psychiatrist, Carl Jung, incorporated into his psychological theories.

Myth: Nobody Changes Unless He Really Wants to Change

QUESTION: "How many psychiatrists does it take to change a light bulb?"

ANSWER: "One, but only if it really wants to change."

Amusing as this joke is, it's oversimplified. People can be *helped* to want to change, through the gentlest support all the way through the most coercive measures. Change is something that happens by degrees. The stages of change model developed by James Prochaska and Carlo DiClemente at the University of Rhode Island defines four stages that people go through when they are making decisions to take a new path:[40]

Precontemplation: not yet ready to change

Contemplation: starting to analyze the pros and cons of change, thinking deeply about the current status quo, owning up to the fact that you are ambivalent (have mixed feelings) about change

Preparation: starting to conceive of the steps you might be able to take to begin the change or new path

Action: going beyond just talking the talk and making the very first step forward

In the case of the person you are trying to help, where "action" means making or attending an appointment with a psychiatrist, there is an internal "cooking" process from precontemplation through preparation. Your efforts help cultivate this process, however slowly. The variety of approaches discussed in this book help to move this process along until, we hope, the other is ready for that last step, action. The message here is to keep trying, keep supporting, keep engaging different measures, bide your time if you can, and remain devoted to the process and the vision of the other's well-being. Changing is a journey, more than a moment of decision.

Once you have gotten your loved one to agree to an evaluation, assuming you are not sitting in the ER, here are things you can do to keep the momentum going.

Come to the Initial Evaluation

If you have been successful in getting the troubled person in your life into a mental health evaluation, offer to go along, perhaps just for moral support. Be sure to introduce yourself to the doctor and offer to join the interview at some point, in order to provide additional observations, history, and other information. Let the doctor know that you will be part of the support system to help the patient cooperate with ongoing appointments. You might be critical in helping both the diagnostic process and cooperation with treatment. You are an additional source of information, what we call an "outside informant."

I teach my residents about the importance of outside informants in diagnosis. Carl's story is one I often share with students.

• **CARL** •

Carl, a forty-five-year-old man, came to get psychiatric help for depression. He looked a mess: dilapidated and in need of a bath and a shave. He was unable to sustain eye contact and stared out the window. He spoke in a monotone, with almost no emotional modulation. He described his anxiety and depression. He lived alone, was unemployed, and had no friends. As I asked him to tell me about his life, he told me that he was a "world famous scientist" who was a theoretical physicist, with solo publications (no co-authors —the most difficult kind of paper to get published) in some of the most prestigious journals in the world. He named an incredibly impressive list for me. He said he had won many scientific awards. In fact, he explained, "I was on the shortlist for the Nobel Prize" at one point. From his appearance and his speech, he really did appear to have a major mental illness like schizophrenia, and these grandiose claims seemed to go along with the delusional psychotic ideas that are typical of such illnesses.

At the end of the evaluation, I agreed to see him again and asked him to sign a release to let me speak to his parents, who lived in San Francisco. He readily agreed. I called them a few days later and told them their son Carl had come to see me in Baltimore, and I wanted to ask them some questions about how long he had been having delusions of being a famous scientist. Before I could ask the question, his mother said, "Poor Carl. Did you know that he was a full professor, a famous scientist, won many awards, and published solo papers in the most prestigious journals for many years? He was even considered for a Nobel Prize at one point!" As improbable as Carl's story initially seemed, it turned out to be all true; his parents were present at each and every step (and I got copies of his scientific papers to satisfy myself). This man was not suffering from a *psychosis, but from a terrible depression that had ruined his career. He was not schizophrenic. Had I not spoken to anyone other than the patient, I would have misdiagnosed him.*

At the Initial Evaluation, Ask Questions

Prepare yourself with questions to ask the evaluator at the time of the initial visit. Many of these ought to be asked by the patient, but sometimes the patient is too ill, upset, or overwhelmed to think of them. You have put yourself in the role of a health care advocate, and these are good questions for an advocate to ask on behalf of a patient. Consider these:

- Is there any more information you need from me?
- What is your conclusion about what is going on?
- What is the diagnosis?
- Is there more than one problem?
- Is there a good book or website to learn more about the condition?
- What is the treatment plan going forward?
- Are you going to treat the patient yourself?
- Are there other specialists who should be involved?
- Will just office visits be enough or is something more called for?
- How often will the visits need to be?
- Is there a penalty for a missed appointment?
- Are you prescribing any medication?
- Where can I read more about the medication?
- What are the possible side effects?
- How will we know it's working?

- How long might it take to work?
- Are there any interactions with other medications or foods to be aware of?
- Are there any specific dos and don'ts to observe as I continue to help?
- Are there other specific instructions, such as:
    - no alcohol?
    - sleep schedule?
    - leave of absence from work?
- What should we do if things get worse?
- How can we contact you in an emergency?
- Can I call you if I observe anything concerning?
- Can you suggest a local support group or agency that helps families and interested others to support someone with this problem?
- If I need help for myself coping with this person's problems, or the changes that might be taking place during treatment, where can I get that?

Continue Your Input after the Initial Evaluation

As seen in the previous list of questions, one of the most vital contributions to good outcomes in psychiatric treatment I have found is a sense of accessibility between the health professional and the person's support system. Each needs to be accessible to the other. In psychiatry, this is a bit tricky, because of confidentiality, which is a venerable and important aspect of treatment. To really open up and reveal one's vulnerable inner life, there has to be a sense of safety; the guarantee of confidentiality helps secure that safety. This means that the patient must give permission to the professional to speak to *anyone* else about the case. Many professionals will get permission to speak with others, as I did in Carl's case.

It is important to know that confidentiality specifically refers to information going *out* of treatment, not *into* treatment. Namely, no law or ethical principle says a doctor needs a patient's permission to *receive* information from others about that patient. So, even if the patient does not give permission for the doctor to speak with you, you can speak *at* the doctor. You can leave a voicemail, write a note, or send an e-mail to express observations and concerns, which can help provide outside information. In fact, if something is very critical and important, like being sure the doctor knows that the patient is drinking alcohol or using drugs, something that a patient may want to hide from the doctor, I suggest you put it in writing. Writing makes things clear. If received by the doctor, it should become part of the written medical record. Having been informed in writing about a significant problem and putting that writing in the medical record elevates it clinically (and legally) to a higher level that is harder for the doctor to neglect.

As previously discussed in chapter 7, remember that some doctors feel it ethically necessary to share those communications from outsiders with their patients. It's therefore best to let the person you are helping know that you have been in touch with the doctor and provided information that you hope can be useful, rather than letting the patient be caught off guard when told by the doctor that you wrote or called. If you attend the initial evaluation, explicitly ask if it would be okay to call or write to the doctor about concerns or observations in the future, as treatment progresses. This will make it clear to the patient from the start that this is an open channel, one that you may well use. If you don't know whether the doctor feels ethically bound to share what you have communicated with the patient, find out *first*, so you know. If you know that what you say will be shared with the patient, you might think twice about what you communicate, or how you put it.

A Change in Them Is a Change for You

We are deeply affected by mental illness and substance abuse in those about whom we care. My work has taught me how amazingly adaptable human beings are to adversity and challenge. Sometimes those adaptations require us to pretzel ourselves into all sorts of awkward functions to cope, even to survive. The better our mental health, the more we can stretch and bend. So it's not unusual for me to observe that living with someone who has a mental illness, or any kind of significant behavioral and/or emotional problem, can really twist you into strange shapes. You

- learn to keep silent about your pain
- walk on eggshells
- "go along to get along"
- avoid the troubled person
- feel ashamed, and withdraw from your own support system
- express your distress "sideways" with passive aggressive push-backs
- displace your frustrations by taking them out on others
- learn to minimize and excuse the other's behaviors, and buy into a shared denial that the problem isn't so bad
- find your own dysfunctional ways to cope, such as with alcohol, drugs, or affairs

- start to internalize your distress and experience physical problems

The list could go on and on. The point is that your relationship is part of a system built around a problem. Solving the problem is going to cause a change in that system, and that means a change for you. You hope, of course, that the immediate benefits of the help your troubled one gets will be positive for you, but be prepared for the possibility that this might not be so—at least not at first. Your troubled other is not the only person who will be changed; you will be, too. If treatment has finally begun, this is a delicate time for you.

Sometimes the support person, the kind of person who is reading this book, consults me after their troubled other starts treatment. Other times, I have witnessed secondhand what happens to the family members, friends, or significant others of my patients as they begin to change. The impact on the support person can be quite disorienting. For example, some people have trouble handling a shift from the troubled other's being in a dominant, aggressive, closed position, to being more dependent, even lost, when he accepts that he has a problem. Or, in the other direction, a needy, passive person starts to become empowered. Either shift can challenge a relationship. Also common is a destabilization in the family that has (up until then) crystallized around a problem; the solving of that problem causes cracks and shifts. For example, I once saw a very stable elderly couple who had lived with their chronically schizophrenic daughter for years suddenly turn hostile on each other when she finally started to get well. The main treatment at that point became marital therapy for the parents, who started to talk about issues that were off the table as long as their focus was on their ill daughter.

What to do in the face of these shifts? Once a diagnosis is made, you can turn to a number of good books for those trying to support people who have psychiatric conditions (see pages 248–251 of the resources section). Good advice is often there about what to expect for specific kinds of illnesses and how to handle changes. Support groups can be especially useful at this time, many of which exist for family and friends, such as those run by the National Alliance on Mental Illness (www.NAMI.com). There is an extensive support group community for people in relationships with alcoholics (Al-Anon) and addicts (Narc-Anon, S-Anon), which acknowledges how painful and twisted relationships can get in these circumstances. These groups aim to empower you in the process of untwisting.

Finally, getting professional support for *yourself* to cope with the pressure of shifts and changes might be valuable. As I've noted, many people have come to me for professional help precisely because they are in this position. In the course of our work, I help educate them about the other's condition, strategize about the changes, and even help them see how they might be contributing to the problem, perhaps enabling it, maybe even exacerbating it.

This last point is a delicate but important one. You have read this far, and so you are probably psychologically minded enough now to consider looking in the mirror. If you've read the earlier chapters, you understand that not all problems in mental life are simply brain diseases. Some can only be understood in the context of a person's environment, including his or her relationships. It is very important to consider the *possibility* that your relationship with the troubled other might be part of the problem, and that your own behaviors could be contributing. Maybe there is more than one troubled person here? Maybe a troubled match between two troubled people? Maybe someone else is reading this book trying to figure out how to approach you? These are difficult but vital questions to ask yourself.

My final tip on this matter is: If the person treating your troubled other invites you to be part of the therapy, or has determined that your relationship needs some help, or even suggests that you yourself get treatment—*do it*. Don't resist it; don't say, "I'm okay, he's the one who needs help." The other is now approaching you to get help in much the same way as you originally approached her! Remember, one of the most important things that a mental health professional provides, other than expertise, is objectivity. (In my opinion, that's worth as much as the expertise.) If an objective professional who has reviewed the total picture thinks your relationship with the troubled other needs attention and help, respond positively to that, just as you have hoped your troubled other would respond positively to all your efforts to get this far.

Once Treatment Begins, Help the Person Stay with It
It is not unusual for me to see patients who have been in mental health treatment before. The majority of those who consult me and explain that prior attempts at treatment did not help very much, eventually reveal they *didn't stick with it* for very long. Whether it was marriage counseling, individual therapy, group therapy, or medications, most of the people who complained of past "treatment failure" had met with a psychiatrist or other clinical therapist fewer than six times. This phenomenon is not limited to my practice experience; studies of so-called treatment failures bear this out. Imagine being prescribed antibiotics for ten days

for a urinary tract infection. After two days you feel better and stop taking the medicine; a couple of days later the symptoms return. Should this be called a failure of antibiotic therapy for the infection? Of course not.

I wish I could tell you that the need for your help was at an end once that initial evaluation has taken place. I do think the *hardest* step has been completed. You have at least gotten the proverbial ball rolling. Once a connection is made with a professional, there is a fairer chance that the patient will remain in treatment, should ongoing treatment be recommended. An expected skill of a mental health professional is trying to secure that connection during the first evaluation. However, studies show that as many as 26 percent of people will not stay in treatment long enough for it to make a difference.[41] On the other hand, in my experience, even if people drop out of treatment too early, it is much easier for them to open that door again in the future, when they are more ready, sometimes because things are worse. As discussed in chapter 3, mental health treatment takes a while, much longer than your typical health care encounter for, say, bronchitis or throwing out your back. The journey is sometimes longer because it may take a few tries at treatment before traction is achieved.

Persist in your support, check in with your person of concern about how the treatment is going, possibly continue accompanying her to appointments for a while where you can greet the professional in the waiting room periodically, and stay part of the process. In this way, the chance that your loved one or friend will be in that large minority of people who drop out will be greatly reduced.

If at First You Don't Succeed . . .

Naturally, almost all the clinical examples I have chosen to put into this book are my success stories. I want you to know that family and friends have not succeeded in the goal of getting that initial evaluation to happen 100 percent of the time. In fact, it is quite common for them to try multiple approaches, gradually going up the scale from the most caring and amiable conversations portrayed in chapter 6, through increasing levels of mobilizing consequences, power, and even ultimately the legal/medical authorities, described in later chapters. So, what if you have tried many of these ideas without success, and the troubled person in your life has not yet gotten that all-important evaluation? Have you exhausted all your options? Obviously, every helper has to decide for herself when she has reached the point of exhaustion and is ready to give up trying. In my experience, however, the more you can sustain the effort, the more likely you are to succeed. Many people have finally come to see me only after a long period of others trying to help them get in. Sometimes, the journey has taken a few years. Occasionally, this happens because one technique or another finally works. Sometimes, it's because things worsen and reach a tipping point. In the recovery community, which focuses on addiction disorders, this is known as "reaching rock bottom." This can involve some kind of emotional or intellectual realization, the proverbial "straw that broke the camel's back." Sometimes, tragically, it involves a catastrophic development (an arrest, a suicide attempt, violence, a significant other leaving, a fatal accident, etc.). It's preferable to prevent catastrophe but, in this business, that is sometimes what it takes.

You may have heard that the average alcoholic or addict goes through treatment and rehab more than once before he finally "gets it" and sustains sobriety. It's also true that other kinds of psychiatric problems may need to be addressed by some or all of the steps in this book a few times before the patient finally participates in treatment or follows treatment recommendations in a meaningful way. As we have seen, many factors can influence someone's readiness for treatment. If those factors are not aligned now, they might well be in the future. You may find yourself in a more advantageous position to influence your loved one. For example, a troubled adult child may have moved home, and therefore your leverage for therapeutic coercion may be stronger. In the future, perhaps the symptoms will have progressed to a level of danger where some of the involuntary and legal approaches described in chapter 9 may work.

The point is, if you find yourself now, at the end of this book, unsuccessful in your goal to help the other get a proper evaluation, don't give up. Maybe you'll give this book to another person who can approach the troubled one from an entirely different angle. Maybe though, you'll put this book on the shelf, and when circumstances change, you will open it again and revisit the steps.

Endure

Hippocrates, who has made a few cameo appearances in this book, practiced medicine and taught in the third century B.C. on the Greek island of Kos. The plane tree under which he taught still lives and has grown to cover over an acre. I visited there and brought back a leaf from that tree, which hangs in my office, casting its shadow over the work I do every day, like its leafy ancestors shaded Hippocrates and his students. Under that leaf I have posted one of Hippocrates's most famous aphorisms: *Ars longa, vita brevis*:

"Skill is long and life is short." To me, this means that persisting with skills, taught to me by my teachers and my patients, will eventually conquer whatever problems I may encounter in those I try to help. The shortness of life and its vicissitudes can be overcome by the application of skill. I invite you, too, to endure, to hold on to the skills that you have acquired from this book, and to stay faithful to the process occurring under the shade of Hippocrates's tree. Trust that the persistent application of your efforts will succeed and the troubled person in your life will accept professional help.

Seven Steps for Convincing a Loved One to Get Help

The following list summarizes the recommended process and methods for convincing a loved one to get help, as well as offering further steps to take should you run into resistance. Use this list as a handy reference guide while putting the different suggestions from this book into practice.

Please note that even though the following list uses the masculine "he" pronoun, this list can apply to both male and female loved ones.

Step 1: Before You Begin

- Know the signs that your loved one's problem is serious enough to need professional help.

- Figure out why you are getting involved, and why it's worth it.

- Understand why he may have avoided getting professional help so far.

- Focus on the goal: Getting a professional mental health evaluation for your loved one.

Step 2: Choose a Time and Place

- Plan in advance a special time and place to speak, to listen, and to discuss the problem with your loved one.

- Avoid discussing the problem at defensive times, family gatherings, holidays, special events, or in the midst of or right after an argument.
- Approach your loved one when everyone is sober.
- Speak with him face-to-face, not by letter, phone, or email.
- Select an emotionally neutral place where he doesn't feel trapped.
- Acknowledge up front that he might be hurt by this discussion.
- Focus your discussion on how you feel affected by your loved one in your discussion.

Step 3: The First Approach

- Let your loved one know you are listening, not just telling him what to do.
- Try to make him feel that it is safe to talk.
- If you feel unsafe, have another person present when you talk with your loved one.
- Be prepared to tolerate your loved one's anger at your concern, but don't let that discourage you.
- Let your loved one have some mixed feelings; he doesn't have to totally agree at first. This is more an ongoing process, than a one-time effort.
- Persist; keep coming back.
- You don't have to figure out what's wrong with your loved one, just communicate *something* is the matter and that a professional can help figure out what, if anything, is the problem.

- Acknowledge to him that you don't have the power yourself to completely help him; you need an experienced trained person to help him, too.
- Be prepared to ask him to get help for your sake, because you need more help to support him.
- Ask him to get an evaluation as a "gift" to you.
- If you have benefited from your own treatment, share that with him.
- Don't be afraid to ask if he has had thoughts of harming himself or ending his life.
- Ask him to consider a single one-time visit at this time; just an "evaluation," not a commitment to "treatment."
- Make the appointment for your loved one (or help him make it) and go with him to the appointment.

Step 4: Gathering Your Allies

- Talk with your loved one's personal physician or other primary care provider about the problem and the need for a psychiatric evaluation. That provider might even be able to provide treatment.
- Consider including in your effort a close sibling, dear friend, or clergy member with whom your loved one has a relationship.
- Even before approaching your loved one, attend a support group meeting for families and friends. Hear the experience and advice of others who have done this.
- Educate yourself about psychiatric problems by reading through memoirs and movies.
- Before approaching your loved one, consult with a psychiatrist or other mental health professional about the problem and how to approach your loved one.

- If you are already getting mental health treatment, let your own care provider help you approach your loved one.

Step 5: Persuasion and Coercion

- Accept that logic doesn't always work.

- Understand how friends and family have more power than any professional or agency.

- Consider privileges that come with responsibilities; in this case, responsibility for your loved one to get help for mental health problems.

- Use the powers of giving or taking away privileges to influence him to get professional help.

- Your relationship with your loved one is important. In serious situations, be prepared to put the relationship at stake, if necessary.

- Consider using the power of a group and gather others for an "intervention."

- Be prepared to deal with those who might be "enablers."

Step 6: "Hardball": Involuntary Evaluation

- Determine if your loved one is dangerous to himself or others.

- Determine if the danger is immediate.

- Know the legal process in your community for involuntary evaluation in the face of immediate dangers.

- If mobilizing the legal steps for involuntary evaluation, show up at each and every step.

- When describing your loved one's situation to authorities, share the most serious behaviors you have seen.

- If he is hospitalized, you may have to close your home to his return, until he is better.
- If he is eligible, consider the VA system.
- Do not be intimidated by fear of damaging the relationship. Not acting can do more damage than acting to mobilize involuntary evaluation.
- If your loved one is already in legal trouble, use that as an opportunity to have the court require psychiatric evaluation and treatment as an outpatient.
- If he is in jail, help to mobilize the psychiatric treatment resources in that facility.
- If he does not have a legal problem, you may have to initiate one; then ask the court to require evaluation and treatment.
- Understand how the legal system treats mental illness and substance abuse differently.
- Protect your own safety and that of children.
- Remove firearms if possible and if it is safe to do so.

Step 7: Continuing Your Support

- Recognize that a crisis isn't necessarily a catastrophe; it is often an opportunity for positive change.
- Do not accept that "nobody changes unless he really wants to."
- Go to the initial evaluation with your loved one and ask specific questions of the professional.
- If there is treatment going forward, continue giving your input to the care provider, even after the evaluation.
- Support your loved one to stick with treatment after it begins.

- Changes in your loved one during treatment may produce changes in you; be prepared to respond to that in yourself and in your relationship with your loved one.

- Consider the possibility that you might benefit from treatment, or your relationship with your loved one might benefit from treatment.

- If you don't succeed in getting your loved one evaluated now, don't give up. There may be a better chance of succeeding later, with further developments.

Websites, Books and Articles, Movies and TV

Mental Health

Support, Information, and Advocacy Organizations

American Psychiatric Association (APA)

www.psych.org

The American Psychiatric Association, founded in 1844, is the world's largest psychiatric organization. It is a medical specialty society representing more than thirty-six thousand psychiatric physicians from the United States and around the world. Its member psychiatrists work together to ensure humane care and effective treatment for all persons with mental disorders, including intellectual developmental disorders and substance use disorders. APA is the main voice of modern psychiatry.

American Psychological Association (APA)

www.apa.org

Based in Washington, DC, the American Psychological Association is a scientific and professional organization that represents psychology in the United States. It is the largest association of psychologists worldwide. The organization's mission is to advance the creation, communication, and application of psychological knowledge to benefit society and improve people's lives.

The Bazelon Center

www.bazelon.org

The Bazelon Center for Mental Health Law is a nonprofit organization devoted to improving the lives of people with mental illnesses through changes in policy and law. Information about involuntary civil commitment procedures in different states can be found here.

The Center for Problem-Oriented Policing (POP)

http://www.popcenter.org/problems/mental_illness

This website addresses education and training of police called to situations in which a person with possible mental illness is behaving threateningly.

Consumer Reports

www.consumerreports.org/health/free-highlights
/manage-your-health/depression/talktherapy.htm

This *Consumer Reports* website has results of a survey about people's experience with mental health treatment. It reviews medication versus talk therapy, how people found the right care provider, their experiences with different types of therapists, and the advantages and disadvantages of using medical insurance to pay for treatment.

Dr. Komrad's Website

www.komradmd.com

On Dr. Komrad's website you can find out more information about him and his practice of psychiatry, listen to samples of his radio and TV interviews, and see a schedule of his upcoming public appearances. He also provides a link to his blog as well as important links to a wide variety of other websites containing information about various psychiatric conditions and resources for support.

Help Connections

www.mhcca.org

This website focuses on mental health and addictions issues in prisons, including guides to how to access treatment while incarcerated. A lengthy and very comprehensive document on these issues can be downloaded at www.nicic.gov/Library/018604.

Mental Health America
(formerly National Mental Health Association)

www.nmha.org

The purposes of Mental Health America are to work for wellness, mental health, and victory over mental and substance use conditions through the development of a coordinated citizens' voluntary movement; to advocate for the improved care and treatment of persons with mental and substance use conditions; to advocate for improved methods and services in research, prevention, detection, diagnosis, and treatment of mental and substance use conditions; to educate the public about mental and substance use conditions and their causes and treatments; and to fight stigma and prejudice.

Mental Health First Aid

www.mentalhealthfirstaid.org/cs

Mental Health First Aid is a groundbreaking public education program that helps the public identify, understand, and respond to signs of mental illnesses and substance use disorders. Mental Health First Aid is offered in the form of an interactive twelve-hour course that presents an overview of mental illness and substance use disorders in the United States, and introduces participants to risk factors and warning signs of mental health problems, builds understanding of their impact, and overviews common treatments.

National Alliance on Mental Illness (NAMI)
www.nami.org

Since 1979, the National Alliance on Mental Illness has been dedicated to improving the lives of individuals and families affected by mental illness through support groups, education, advocacy, and research. The organization's "Family-to-Family" education series is a free twelve-week course for family caregivers of individuals with mental illnesses. Family-to-Family classes are offered in hundreds of communities across the country, taught by trained family members who have struggled and developed experience with their own mentally ill family members.

National Association of Social Workers (NASW)
www.socialworkers.org

The National Association of Social Workers is the largest membership organization of professional social workers in the world. NASW works to enhance the professional growth and development of its members, to create and maintain professional standards, and to advance sound social policies.

National Federation of Families for Children's Mental Health (NFFCMH)
www.ffcmh.org

This national family-run organization focuses on issues of children and youth with emotional, behavioral, or other mental health needs and their families.

Review of "Involuntary Commitment"
http://en.wikipedia.org/wiki/Involuntary_commitment

The Wikipedia entry on "involuntary commitment" is a fairly accurate and comprehensive review of this concept, both in the United States and abroad. It also has specific information about certain states. Its links to related topics on Wikipedia and to other reliable websites are especially useful.

The Treatment Advocacy Center

www.treatmentadvocacycenter.org

The Treatment Advocacy Center is a national nonprofit organization dedicated to eliminating barriers to the timely and effective treatment of severe mental illness. The organization promotes laws, policies, and practices for the delivery of psychiatric care and supports the development of innovative treatments for and research into the causes of severe and persistent psychiatric illnesses, such as schizophrenia and bipolar disorder. Resources and information on getting help for a loved one can be found under the "Get Help" tab on the homepage.

Government Organizations

Americans with Disabilities Act (ADA)

www.ada.gov

This site, run by the U.S. Department of Justice, reviews the federal law concerning the rights of disabled Americans (including those with mental illness).

National Institute of Mental Health (NIMH)

www.nimh.nih.gov

The mission of the National Institute of Mental Health is to transform the understanding and treatment of mental illnesses through basic and clinical research, paving the way for prevention, recovery, and cure. This is one of the best sources of information about a wide variety of psychiatric problems and research efforts being made (and funded by the U.S. government) to treat them.

U.S. Department of Health and Human Services (HHS): Substance Abuse and Mental Health Services Administration (SAMHSA)

www.samhsa.gov

The Substance Abuse and Mental Health Services Administration's mission is to reduce the impact of substance abuse and mental illness on America's communities. SAMHSA's information on the prevention of mental illness and substance abuse is particularly notable.

U.S. Department of Veterans Affairs Mental Health
www.mentalhealth.va.gov

This site has information specific to mental health issues and resources for veterans.

Addiction Treatment

Al-Anon
www.al-anon.alateen.org

The official site of the worldwide Twelve Step organization for families of those with addictions.

Alcoholics Anonymous (AA)
www.aa.org

The official site of the Twelve Step worldwide organization to help alcoholics maintain sobriety.

Co-Dependents Anonymous (CoDA)
www.coda.org

The official site of the worldwide Twelve Step organization for people who have lost themselves in emotionally troubled relationships.

Hazelden Foundation
www.hazelden.org

Hazelden helps individuals, families, and communities struggling with alcohol abuse, substance abuse, and drug addiction to transform their lives.

Narcotics Anonymous (NA)

www.na.org

The official site of the Twelve Step worldwide organization for addicts who wish to find a new way of life.

National Alcoholism and Substance Abuse Information Center (NASAIC)

www.addictioncareoptions.com

This website includes a locator for local treatment programs in each state.

Domestic Violence

National Coalition Against Domestic Violence (NCADV)

www.ncadv.org/resources/StateCoalitionList.php

This is an advocacy organization and educational clearinghouse of information about resources for domestic violence. It provides a state-by-state list of affiliates who will help connect you to treatment, support, and legal resources in your area.

Suicide Prevention

National Suicide Prevention Lifeline

www.suicidepreventionlifeline.org

1-800-273-TALK (8255)

This twenty-four-hour, toll-free, confidential suicide prevention hotline is available to anyone in suicidal crisis or emotional distress. Crisis counseling and mental health referrals are provided day and night.

Books and Articles

Helping Those with Psychiatric Conditions and Addictions

Alcoholics Anonymous: The Big Book, 4th ed. Alcoholics Anonymous World Services, 2002.

Amador, Xavier. *I Am Not Sick, I Don't Need Help! How to Help Someone with Mental Illness Accept Treatment*. Vida Press, 2007.

Aviv, Rachel. "God Knows Where I Am: What Should Happen When Patients Reject Their Diagnosis." *The New Yorker,* May 30, 2011.

Carter, Rosalynn, and Susan Golant. *Helping Someone with Mental Illness: A Compassionate Guide for Family, Friends, and Caregivers.* Three Rivers Press, 1999.

Carter, Rosalynn, and Susan Golant. *Helping Yourself Help Others: A Book for Caregivers.* Random House, 1994.

Fast, Julie, and John D. Preston. *Loving Someone with Bipolar Disorder.* New Harbinger Press, 2004.

Golant, Mitch, and Susan Golant. *What to Do When Someone You Love Is Depressed: A Self-Help and Help Others Guide.* Villard, 1996.

Hornbacher, Marya. *Sane: Mental Illness, Addiction, and the Twelve Steps.* Hazelden, 2010.

Jamison, Kay. *Night Falls Fast: Understanding Suicide.* Vintage, 2000.

Jay, Jeff, and Debra Jay. *Love First: A Family's Guide to Intervention,* 2nd ed. Hazelden, 2008.

Kelly, Kate, and Peggy Ramundo. *You Mean I'm Not Lazy, Stupid or Crazy?! The Classic Self-Help Book for Adults with Attention Deficit Disorder.* Scribner, 2006.

Komrad, Mark. "A Defense of Medical Paternalism: Maximizing Patients' Autonomy." *Journal of Medical Ethics,* 9 (1983): 33–44. (Now reprinted widely in many textbooks of medical ethics.)

Kreger, Randi, and Paul Mason. *Stop Walking on Eggshells: Taking Your Life Back When Someone You Care about Has Borderline Personality Disorder.* New Harbinger, 2010.

Mace, Nancy, and Peter Rabins. *The 36-Hour Day: A Family Guide to Caring for People with Alzheimer Disease, Other Dementias, and Memory Loss in Later Life,* 4th ed. Johns Hopkins University Press, 2006.

McGovern, Mark. *Living with Co-occurring Disorders: A Handbook for Recovery.* Hazelden, 2009.

Meyers, Robert, and Brenda Wolf. *Get Your Loved One Sober: Alternatives to Nagging, Pleading, and Threatening.* Hazelden, 2003.

Moore, Joseph. *Helping Skills for the Nonprofessional Counselor.* St. Anthony Messenger Press, 1991.

Real, Terrence. *I Don't Want to Talk About It: Overcoming the Secret Legacy of Male Depression.* Fireside, 1997.

Rosen, Laura, and Xavier Amador. *When Someone You Love Is Depressed.* Free Press, 1996.

Torrey, E. Fuller. *Surviving Schizophrenia: A Manual for Families, Patients, and Providers,* 5th ed. Harper, 2006.

Torrey, E. Fuller and Michael Knable. *Surviving Manic Depression: A Manual on Bipolar Disorder for Patients, Families, and Providers.* Basic Books, 2005.

Training Families to Do a Successful Intervention. Hazelden, 1996.

When Someone You Care About Abuses Drugs and Alcohol: When to Act, What to Say. Hazelden, 1993. (pamphlet)

Woititz, Janet. *Adult Children of Alcoholics.* HCI, 1990.

Woolis, Rebecca. *When Someone You Love Has a Mental Illness.* Penguin, 2003.

Zabawa, Mark Allen. *A Restful Mind: Daily Meditations for Enhancing Mental Health.* Hazelden, 2010.

Psychiatry

Carlat, Daniel. *Unhinged: The Trouble with Psychiatry—A Doctor's Revelations about a Profession in Crisis.* Free Press, 2010.

Frank, Jerome, and Julia Frank. *Persuasion and Healing: A Comparative Study of Psychotherapy.* Johns Hopkins University Press, 1993.

McHugh, Paul. *The Mind Has Mountains.* Johns Hopkins University Press, 2005.

McHugh, Paul, and Phillip Slavney. *The Perspectives of Psychiatry.* Johns Hopkins University Press, 1998.

Miller, Dinah, Annette Hanson, and Steven Daviss. *Shrink Rap: Three Psychiatrists Explain Their Work.* Johns Hopkins University Press, 2011. (This book is associated with an excellent podcast and blog: www.psychiatrist-blog.blogspot.com/.)

Torrey, E. Fuller. *Freudian Fraud: The Malignant Effect of Freudian Theory on American Culture.* Lucas Books, 1999.

The Mentally Ill and Society

Carter, Rosalynn, Susan Golant, and Kathryn Cade. *Within Our Reach: Ending the Mental Health Crisis.* Rodale, 2010.

Earley, Pete. *Crazy: A Father's Search Through America's Mental Health Madness.* Berkley Trade, 2007.

Hinshaw, Stephen. *The Mark of Shame: Stigma of Mental Illness and an Agenda for Change.* Oxford University Press, 2007.

Communication and Dialogue

Bernstein, Albert. *How to Deal with Emotionally Explosive People.* Mcgraw-Hill, 2002.

Rollnick, Stephen, and William Miller. *Motivational Interviewing in Health Care: Helping Patients Change Behavior.* Guilford Press, 2006.

Stone, Douglas, Bruce Patton, and Sheila Heen. *Difficult Conversations: How to Discuss What Matters Most.* Penguin, 2010.

Tannen, Deborah. *You Just Don't Understand: Women and Men in Conversation.* William Morrow, 2001.

Ury, William. *Getting Past No.* Bantam, 1993.

Memoirs and Biography

Beers, Clifford. *A Mind That Found Itself: A Memoir of Madness and Recovery.* CreateSpace, 2009.

Bell, Jeff. *Rewind, Replay, Repeat: A Memoir of Obsessive-Compulsive Disorder.* Hazelden, 2007.

Blauner, Susan. *How I Stayed Alive When My Brain Was Trying to Kill Me: One Person's Guide to Suicide Prevention.* William Morrow, 2002.

Cronkite, Kathy. *On the Edge of Darkness: Celebrated Actors, Journalists and Politicians Chronicle Their Most Arduous Journey.* Delta, 1995.

Davis, Tom. *A Legacy of Madness: Recovering My Family from Generations of Mental Illness.* Hazelden, 2011.

Dukakis, Kitty, and Jane Scovell. *Now You Know.* Simon & Schuster, 1992.

Dukakis, Kitty, and Larry Tye. *Shock: The Healing Power of Electroconvulsive Therapy.* Avery Trade, 2007.

Duke, Patty, and Gloria Hochman. *Brilliant Madness: Living with Manic Depressive Illness.* Bantam, 1992.

Fisher, Carrie. *Shockaholic.* Simon & Schuster, 2011.

Griffin, Peter. *When You Hear the Bugle Call: Battling PTSD and the Unraveling of the American Conscience.* Trafford, 2006.

Hammond, Darrell. *God, If You Are Not Up There, I'm F*cked: Tales of Stand-up Comedy, Saturday Night Live, and other Mind-Altering Mayhem.* Harper, 2011.

Hornbacher, Marya. *Wasted: A Memoir of Anorexia and Bulemia.* Harper Perennial, 2006.

Jamison, Kay. *An Unquiet Mind: A Memoir of Moods and Madness.* Vintage, 1997.

Manning, Martha. *Undercurrents: A Therapist's Reckoning with Depression.* Harper, 1995.

Nasar, Sylvia. *A Beautiful Mind: A Biography of John Forbes Nash, Jr.* Simon & Schuster, 2011.

Radano, Gerry. *Contaminated: My Journey Out of Obsessive Compulsive Disorder.* Bar-Le-Duc, 2007.

Reiland, Rachel. *Get Me Out of Here: My Recovery from Borderline Personality Disorder.* Hazelden, 2004.

Rogers, Barb. *If I Die Before I Wake: A Memoir of Drinking and Recovery.* Conari, 2010.

Saks, Elyn. *The Center Cannot Hold: My Journey Through Madness.* Hyperion, 2008.

Saxen, Ron. *The Good Eater: One Man's Struggle with Binge Eating Disorder.* New Harbinger, 2007.

Sedgwick, John. *In My Blood: Six Generations of Madness and Desire in an American Family.* Harper Perennial, 2008.

Sheff, David. *Beautiful Boy: A Father's Journey Through His Son's Addiction.* Mariner Books, 2009.

Shenk, Joshua. *Lincoln's Melancholy: How Depression Challenged a President and Fueled His Greatness.* Martiner Books, 2005.

Silverman, Sue. *Love Sick: One Woman's Journey Through Sexual Addiction.* W. W. Norton, 2008.

Solomon, Andrew. *The Noonday Demon: An Atlas of Depression.* Scribner, 2002.

Stecker, Tracy. *5 Survivors: Personal Stories of Healing from PTSD and Traumatic Events.* Hazelden, 2011.

Styron, William. *Darkness Visible: A Memoir of Madness.* Modern Library, 2007.

Thompson, Tracy. *The Beast: A Journey Through Depression.* Plume, 1996.

Walls, Jeannette. *The Glass Castle: A Memoir.* Scribner, 2006.

Movies and TV

Former First Lady Rosalynn Carter often points to the film *Ordinary People* as an exemplary positive portrayal of a psychiatrist and psychiatric treatment. Personally, I like the movie that I helped script and on which I advised the director and actors: *Silent Fall*. In that film, given the opportunity to have sex with his patient's sister, the psychiatrist, played by Richard Dreyfuss, correctly holds the professional boundary and refuses. Though flawed, some movies have positive portrayals of therapy and outcomes, like *Ordinary People* and *Good Will Hunting. The Sopranos* at least portrayed the psychiatrist, Dr. Melfi, as compassionate, devoted, and intelligent (if not very effective).

The HBO series *In Treatment* at least accurately shows what a therapy dialogue between a psychiatrist and patient is like; although, in a month of my real practice, I have maybe only three such interesting, penetrating, and dramatic sessions as any one episode of *In Treatment*! The truth is, ordinary psychiatric treatment is quite mundane and routine, dramatic breakthroughs are far between, and improvements happen by slow degrees. Movies usually don't show these aspects of treatment. Occasionally, treatment is dramatic, the hour is stunning, and the turnaround is amazing, but this isn't everyday practice. Movies might lead you to believe that all effective therapy eventually comes to a head when the patient remembers or can speak about some previously unspeakable trauma, has a strong emotional reaction, expresses vulnerable feelings never expressed before, and has a "breakthrough" in emotional well-being because of such a "confession." There is seldom a single or dramatic turning point in a case. People get better by various other means, such as gradually trying new behaviors, learning a new communication skill, or just taking their meds. One rarely sees psychiatric medication offered to patients in movies—unless it's to threaten, restrain, or torture them!

After the release of the movie *Prince of Tides*, I was bewildered to receive half a dozen calls from people seeking treatment. Although most psychiatrists did not like how Barbra Streisand portrayed us (curiously, many were offended by her long, manicured fingernails!), many viewers found the portrayal of psychiatric treatment compelling and inviting. Apparently, this was a sufficiently positive portrayal that it inspired many people who had been contemplating seeking help to pick up the phone. I immediately had to refute the image of psychiatric treatment that these callers saw in that movie (i.e., it's *not* acceptable for psychiatrist and patient to have sexual relations, as shown in the movie!).

I want to address one movie that stands out as one of the most egregious contributors to misinformation about psychiatry: *One Flew Over the Cuckoo's Nest*. This movie shows one of the most healing treatments in psychiatry: electroconvulsive therapy (ECT), sometimes referred to in popular culture by the unfortunate term "shock therapy." The movie portrays ECT as a punishment for a patient's bad behavior (the movie's anti-hero, Randle Patrick McMurphy). ECT was never (properly) used in this way. ECT is also depicted as a punishment in *The Changeling*. I can't say for sure that ECT as punishment never happened, but that kind of abuse was never an accepted practice, as it seemed to be in these movies. Secondly, the method of administering ECT that was depicted in *Cuckoo's Nest* was already twenty years out of date at the time the movie was made (1975). Instead of showing the far less dramatic use of general anesthesia, supported breathing by the anesthetist, and the use of muscle relaxants (to avoid a convulsion), the movie depicted ECT as it was in the 1940s, grossly distorting an important treatment.

Over the course of my two decades in this field, I have recommended ECT to hundreds of patients. Sadly, some have refused because of the frightening images in *Cuckoo's Nest* (I know this because they told me so!), and I could not talk them out of their fear. Two went on to die from depression because they refused the only potentially life-saving (and safe) treatment—ECT—that could have helped their difficult cases. I have heard too many similar stories from colleagues, which is why I see *One Flew Over the Cuckoo's Nest* as the most dangerous film in the history of psychiatry.

Here are a few movies or TV programs that, though somewhat flawed, come the closest to accurate portrayals of mental illness and psychiatric treatment:

Alcoholism: *Affliction, Days of Wine and Roses*

Anorexia: *Dying to Dance*

Anxiety Disorder: *Annie Hall*

Bipolar Disorder: *Mr. Jones*

Borderline Personality Disorder: *Girl Interrupted, Fatal Attraction*

Bulimia: *Freeway II: Confessions of a Trickbaby*

Cocaine Abuse: *Blow*

Compulsive Personality Disorder: *As Good As It Gets*

Narcissistic Personality Disorder: *Wall Street*

Panic Disorder: *Analyze This*

Post-traumatic Stress Disorder: *In Country, Born on the Fourth of July*

Psychotherapy: HBO's *In Treatment*

Schizophrenia: *A Beautiful Mind*

To find additional movies related to individual psychiatric conditions:

Reel Psychiatry: Movie Portrayals of Psychiatric Conditions. David Robinson. Rapid Psychler Press, 2003.

Movies and Mental Illness: Using Films to Understand Psychopathology, 3rd ed. Danny Wedding, Mary Ann Boyd, and Ryan M. Niemiec. Hogrefe, 2010.

www.fanlight.com
Fanlight Productions is a leading distributor of innovative films and video works on the social issues of our time, with a special focus on health care, mental health, professional ethics, aging and gerontology, disabilities, the workplace, and gender and family issues.

Documentaries

Suicide: *The Bridge*

Teen Depression: *Cry for Help*

Mental Illness and Stigma: *No Kidding: Me 2* (a documentary by actor Joe Pantoliano, including discussion of his own depression)

Schizophrenia: *Out of the Shadow*

Depression: *Out of the Shadows* (similar to above title, but a different movie)

Depression: *Dead Blue*

Mental Illness, Stigma, Recovery and Hope: *Shadow Voices: Finding Hope in Mental Illness*

People with Mental Illness Speak About Their Lives: *Fine Line: Mental Health / Mental Illness*

Addiction: HBO series of documentary films on addiction, available at www.hbo.com/addiction/thefilm

Journey of Recovery / Recovering from Mental Illness / Documentary Educational Video. (film available on YouTube) http://www.youtube.com/watch?v=XUKhMJyupa8

Finding Professional Help

American Psychiatric Association

One of the most direct ways to find a psychiatrist in your area is to contact your state's district branch of the American Psychiatric Association (www.psych.org/dblisting). Almost all have a referral service, with listings of psychiatrists and their interests and specializations.

American Psychological Association

http://locator.apa.org

The American Psychological Association website can give you a listing of psychologists who practice in your area. You can even specify the specific kind of problem for which you are seeking help.

Childhood Protective Services in Your State

http://pediatrics.about.com/cs/childabuse/a/reporting_abuse.htm

Find a Therapist.com

www.find-a-therapist.com

Search through Find-a-Therapist's directory of verified therapists, psychologists, marriage and family counselors, social workers, licensed professional counselors, and psychiatrists.

Financial Aid for Treatment

Applying for Medicaid (for low-income individuals) or Medicare (for disabled individuals) is not as hard as it seems. If someone is mentally impaired, a family member, friend, or other advocate can represent the person and walk him or her through the process. The place to begin is the local Social Security office, which can initiate the application for either Medicaid or Medicare or both. Often, the local CMHC (community mental health clinic) can start seeing the troubled person on a sliding-scale fee schedule, and a social worker in the clinic will help with the application process.

Many mental health professionals in private clinics and group practices provide sliding-scale fees based on income. In many states, the state psychiatric association encourages psychiatrists to take on a handful of cases for free or at minimal cost, just as most law firms ask members to give some pro bono time. To find the number of your state psychiatric association, call the American Psychiatric Association at 1-888-35-PSYCH or visit www.psych.org. It has become increasingly common for medical schools and training hospitals to allow their trainees (psychiatric residents) to treat people for free. Check with the department of psychiatry at your nearest medical school about such programs at teaching facilities in your area.

Finding a Professional to Help Plan an Intervention

A good clearinghouse for finding trained interventionists in your area is the National Alcoholism and Substance Abuse Information Center, which can make referrals for interventions to address general psychiatric problems in addition to substance abuse problems (www.addictioncareoptions.com). Also, the National Intervention for Drugs and Alcohol maintains a database to find licensed interventionists throughout the United States who can help families plan an intervention (www.interventiondrugsandalcohol.org).

National Alcoholism and Substance Abuse Information Center
www.addictioncareoptions.com

Includes a locator for local treatment programs in each state.

National Council for Community Behavioral Healthcare
www.thenationalcouncil.org/cs/about_us

To locate mental health, behavioral health, and addictions treatment organizations in your community, use Find a Provider under the Press & Public dropdown menu.

The Nearest Medical School

Call the medical school closest to your home, and ask to be connected with the Department of Psychiatry. These departments all have resources to help refer you to one of the mental health professionals on their faculty. Also, the hospitals associated with the medical schools have various services to provide emergency or urgent evaluations for patients. Often there is a clinic run by psychiatric residents in training that provides treatment for free or minimal cost.

The Nearest Mental Health Treatment Facility
www.ushospital.info/Psychiatric.htm

This website provides a directory of mental health treatment centers in every state.

Mental Health Treatment for Veterans
www.mentalhealth.va.gov/gethelp.asp

Psychology Today
www.psychologytoday.com

This is the website for America's most popular magazine about psychology. Click on Find a Therapist at the top of the page.

Notes

1. P. McHugh and P. Slavney, *The Perspectives of Psychiatry* (Baltimore: Johns Hopkins University Press, 1998).

2. R. C. Kessler, W. T. Chiu, O. Demler, and E. E. Walters, "Prevalence, Severity, and Comorbidity of 12-Month DSM-IV Disorders in the National Comorbidity Survey Replication," *Archives of General Psychiatry* 62, no. 6 (2005): 617–27.

3. National Institutes of Health, "The Numbers Count: Mental Disorders in America." wwwapps.nimh.nih.gov/health/publications/the-numbers-count-mental-disorders-in-america.shtml#Major Depressive.

4. N. Carpenter, "Depression Looms in the Third World," *De Morgen* (Sept. 4, 1999): 17. Also, World Health Organization: www.who.int/mental_health/management/depression/definition/en.

5. E. Messias, W. Eaton, G. Nestadt, O. J. Bienvenu, and J. Samuels, "Psychiatrists' Ascertained Treatment Needs for Mental Disorders in a Population Based Sample," *Psychiatric Services* 58 (2007): 373–77.

6. J. Pagura, S. Fotti, L. Katz, and J. Sareen, "Help Seeking and Perceived Need for Mental Health Care among Individuals in Canada with Suicidal Behaviors," *Psychiatric Services* 60, no. 7 (2009): 943–49.

7. P. S. Wang, M. Lane, M. Olfson, H. A. Pincus, K. B. Wells, and R. C. Kessler, "Twelve-Month Use of Mental Health Services in the United States," *Archives of General Psychiatry* 62 (2005): 629–40.

8. National Institutes of Health, "The Numbers Count: Mental Disorders in America." wwwapps.nimh.nih.gov/health/publications/the-numbers-count-mental-disorders-in-america.shtml#Major Depressive.

9. American Association of Suicidology: www.suicidology.org.

10. "American Roulette: Murder-Suicide in the United States," (Washington, DC: Violence Policy Center, May 2006).

11. M. Hansen, "Safe Haven Meant Kids Finally Got Right Help," *Omaha World-Herald* (Feb. 1, 2009).

12. J. Warner, "Children in the Mental Health Void," *New York Times Opinionator* (Feb. 19, 2009). http://opinionator.blogs.nytimes. com/2009/02/19/is-there-no-place-on-earth.

13. R. C. Kessler, S. Heeringa, M. D. LaKoma, M. Petukhova, A. E. Rupp, M. Schoenbaum, P. S. Wang, and A. M. Zaslavsky, "Individual and Societal Effects of Mental Disorders on Earnings in the United States: Results from the National Comorbidity Survey Replication," *American Journal of Psychiatry* 165 (2008): 703–11.

14. T. Zwillich, "Child Suicide Risk: Assess Parents," *Clinical Psychiatric News* (June 1998): 18.

15. Centers for Disease Control, "Alcohol Use FastStats," (2009), www. cdc.gov/nchs/fastats/alcohol.htm.

16. M. Elias, "Depressed Parents' Negative Effects on Children Are Combatable," *Los Angeles Times* (Mar. 15, 2010).

17. J. Monahan, H. J. Steadman, E. Silver, P. S. Appelbaum, P. Clark Robbins, E. P. Mulvey, L. H. Roth, T. Grisso, and S. Banks, *Rethinking Risk Assessment: The MacArthur Study of Mental Disorder and Violence* (Oxford: Oxford University Press, 2001).

18. E. F. Torrey, "A Predictable Tragedy in Arizona," *Wall Street Journal* (Jan. 12, 2011).

19. D. M. Steinwachs, J. D. Kasper, and E. A. Skinner, *Final Report: NAMI Family Survey* (Arlington, VA: National Alliance on Mental Illness, 1992).

20. M. Hughes, M. Brymer, W. T. Chiu, J. A. Fairbank, R. T. Jones, R. S. Pynoos, V. Rothwell, A. M. Steinberg, and R. C. Kessler, "Posttraumatic Stress among Students after the Shooting at Virginia Tech," *Psychological Trauma: Theory, Research, Practice and Policy* 3, no. 4 (2011): 403–11.

21. National Institute of Mental Health, "Suicide in the U.S.: Statistics and Prevention." wwwapps.nimh.nih.gov/health/publications/suicide-in-the-us-statistics-and-prevention.shtml.

22. J. Cradock-O'Leary, A. S. Young, E. M. Yano, M. Wang, and M. L. Lee, "Use of General Medical Services by VA Patients with Psychiatric Disorders," *Psychiatric Services* 53 (2002): 874–78.

23. R. Aviv, "God Knows Where I Am: What Should Happen When Patients Reject their Diagnosis," *The New Yorker* (May 30, 2011): 57.

24. C. Jung, *Dream Analysis*, vol. 3 (Princeton, NJ: Princeton University Press, 1984): 26.

25. R. Carter and S. Golant, *Helping Someone with Mental Illness* (New York: Three Rivers Press, 1999): 228.

26. G. Gerbner, "Images that Hurt: Mental Illness in the Mass Media," *Journal of the California Alliance of the Mentally Ill* 4, no. 1 (1993): 17.

27. J. Fink and A. Tasman, *Stigma and Mental Illness* (Washington, DC: American Psychiatric Press, 1992).

28. Survey of Men's Health by *Men's Health* magazine and CNN for National Men's Health Week, 1999.

29. R. Spitzer, J. B. Williams, K. Kroenke, M. Linzer, F. V. deGruy, S. R. Hahn, D. Brody, and J. G. Johnson, "Utility of a New Procedure for Diagnosing Mental Disorders in Primary Care: The PRIME-MD 1000 Study," *Journal of the American Medical Association* 272 (1994): 1749–56.

30. J. Coyne, T. L. Schwenk, and S. Fechner-Bates, "Nondetection of Depression by Primary Care Physicians Reconsidered," *General Hospital Psychiatry* 17 (1995): 3–12.

31. Department of Health and Human Services, "Obama Administration Issues Rules Requiring Parity in Treatment of Mental, Substance Use Disorders," www.hhs.gov/news/press/2010pres/01/20100129a.html.

32. Mental Health America, *Ranking America's Mental Health: An Analysis of Depression across the States*, www.nmha.org/go/state-ranking.

33. D. Carlat, *Unhinged: The Trouble with Psychiatry—A Doctor's Revelations about a Profession in Crisis* (New York: Free Press, 2010): 201.

34. www.nimh.nih.gov/statistics

35. "Mental Health: Does Therapy Help?" *Consumer Reports,* November 1995.

36. E. F. S. Kaner, F. Beyer, H. O. Dickinson, E. Pienaar, F. Campbell, C. Schlesinger, N. Heather, J. Saunders, and B. Burnand, "Effectiveness of Brief Alcohol Interventions in Primary Care Populations," *Cochrane Database of Systematic Reviews* 2 (2007): CD004148.

37. The Sentencing Project, *Mentally Ill Offenders in the Criminal Justice System: An Analysis and Prescription* (January 2002). www.sentencingproject.org/doc/publications/sl_mentallyilloffenders.pdf

38. L. Gater, "Prison Mental Health Treatment: Trying to Keep Up with the Outside World," *Corrections Forum* 20, no. 1 (2011): 16–21.

39. M. Miller and D. Hemenway, "Guns and Suicide in the U.S.," *New England Journal of Medicine* 359 (2008): 989–91.

40. J. Prochaska, C. DiClemente, and J. Norcross, "In Search of How People Change: Applications to Addictive Behaviors," *American Psychologist* 47, no. 9 (September 1992): 1102–14.

41. E. Tehrani, J. Krussel, L. Borg, and P. Munk-Jorgensen, "Dropping Out of Psychiatric Treatment: A Prospective Study of a First-Admission Cohort," *Acta Psychiatrica Scandinavica* 94, no. 4 (1996): 266–71.

About the Author

Mark Komrad, M.D. is a psychiatrist with more than twenty-five years of experience treating depression, anxiety, personality disorders, substance abuse, and major mental illness. In addition, he consults with people struggling to convince a loved one who is having emotional or behavioral problems to get professional help. While hosting a nationally syndicated radio talk show about psychiatry, Dr. Komrad helped millions of listeners. He is a regular guest on National Public Radio and on television, discussing a variety of psychiatric issues and providing guidance on helping loved ones get the treatment they need. As a teacher and consultant in psychiatric ethics, Dr. Komrad has worked with Hollywood film and television directors to help them portray mental disorders and psychiatrists more accurately and ethically. He practices psychiatry in Baltimore, MD, where he lives with his wife and son. You can find him on the Internet at www.komradmd.com.